Ordinary Miracles

Dorothy A. Day

Copyright 2023 © Dorothy A. Day

All rights reserved.

No part of this book may be reproduced, stored in a retrieval system, or transmitted by any means, electronic, mechanical, photocopying, recording, or otherwise, without written permission from the author.

ISBN (Paperback): 979-8-9886154-5-3
ISBN (Hardcover): 979-8-9886154-6-0
ISBN (eBook): 979-8-9886154-4-6

DEDICATION

Years ago, the late, great anthropologist Margaret Mead defined the first evidence of civilization in an ancient creature as a broken and healed femur or thighbone. The healing indicates someone took the time to bind the wound, carry the sufferer to safety, and tend to his needs long enough for recovery. Civilization starts with helping and serving others. Fred Rogers of "Mr. Rogers's Neighborhood" told us and the children,
"Look for the helpers."

This collection of eclectic pieces pays homage to the helpers, the miracle workers of the ordinary acts making life a little better for each of us. Many shared because of their own or Jesus' woundedness. Others told of life's little events with God's fingerprint of His goodness and provision touching.
May their examples inspire us.

For the miracle workers.

"Do unto others what you would have them do unto you."
Luke 6:32

ACKNOWLEDGMENTS

I have a novel in me wanting to escape. But, to have the skill and discipline to bring it out, I needed help to hone and polish further my writing and learn the truth of staying at the task. My efforts alone would make a slim volume. However, Johnny Lowe taught me how to put together an anthology, and I used his editorial work, *Virtues of the Heart,* for my example.

Some of the people from whom I begged pieces were generous professional authors. Others were friends who didn't say "no" to my plea to share their stories. Former students also shared, as did Facebook friends with whom I had rekindled long-ago relationships. I have been trusted, an humbling experience. They are my miracle-workers, tellers of tales I'm so proud and honored to use.

The group most responsible for helping me learn to write better were members of the Mid-Mississippi Writers Guild who formed the Madison Critique Group: Lottie Brent Boggan, Reni Bumpas, Gerald and Reva Daniel, Hazel Lonie, Janet Taylor-Perry, Patricia Roberts, and Terry Woosley. I must heed their instructions to show, not tell.

The Gleaners, another group of women, including some who provided stories, furnished caring and support through prayer, visits, food offerings, and understanding when I turned down invitations.

As muscular dystrophy progressed, my typing skills regressed. I asked friends for referrals to someone who typed. Barbara Grillot Gaddy asked, "Will I do?" Her resume was not needed, and she would definitely do. This book would not exist without her typing, proofing, editing, and formatting abilities. What a godsend, miracle-maker, and friend she has been!

Last, my family. I was buoyed by their encouragement and love. I purloined some of my grands' school efforts or their stories. But, Charles — without him, I would not be clean, or dressed, toileted or transported, or so loved. Love really is an action word. He picks me up to transfer approximately twelve times daily, too much for any one person, but particularly someone of our age — 73. He no longer has me to help with the chores we once shared. In addition to house, vehicle, and yard maintenance, Charles has added on laundry, cooking, house cleaning, and caring for me. For over fifty years he has honored the "till death doth thee part" vows. I have been cherished. I have been cared for. He is a miracle maker; he is a miracle.

Cover photography by Jasmin Berry Clark — Jasography

AGAPE OUTREACH MISSION — INDIA

India is a country closed to foreign missionaries; any foreigner who is speaking the gospel news there has lied to the government about his purpose for being there. Not only is it closed, but it is a hostile environment to the Christian gospel and its congregants.

Proponents of Hinduism desire to make India a Hindu country. They use many of the tactics used by radical Muslims in Africa and Asia. There are frequent reports of murderous and other attacks; burning literature, physical assault, destruction of equipment, interruption of meetings all over the country. Christians are persecuted and martyred in India.

The American Bible Society Bible-smugglers set up meetings to distribute Bibles in clearings out in the country. Sometimes they receive word someone has infiltrated their group, and the meeting is compromised. They go on to the next meeting.

The country is now led by one who believes the entire country should be Hindu, and the hostility has ramped up. The caste system is set in place; the castes above you are your superiors; the ones below you are your inferiors. Even below the lowest caste are the untouchables, numbering around 200 million people.

With Hinduism there is a striving to appease wrathful gods and goddesses; many believe purifying the state part of the religion will eliminate suffering and ensure prosperity.

Why, on earth, would anyone voluntarily go to this nation to hug untouchables, to bring living water? Why would people risk not only their own lives but also the lives of their families?

An American can live in India as a rich man for not much money. But to go and tell and risk that martyrdom ... incredible!

Two who go are Americans by adoption, born in India. They are Mississippi residents who go into India as church planters six months of each year and return home to America to raise support the other six. They are members of a Southern Baptist church.

The Lord used the Covid lockdown to teach them how to minister to larger groups via video. They support with their ministry over fifty gospel workers each month; they, by raising funds through individuals and churches, seek to complete three church buildings under construction in India, and a children's hostel as the government issues no permits for orphanages.

Recently two more people-group areas have opened for evangelizing and planting churches. Although these places have several volunteer gospel workers, they need support to reach out to pioneer areas. They need funds for travel, food, literature, and megaphones.

They go and tell because of Jesus' love.

A portion of the proceeds of this book will be donated to Agape Outreach Mission [P.O. Box 3883, Brookhaven, Mississippi 39603]. May God multiply His people through their obedience to "Go and tell."

TABLE OF CONTENTS

Della's Cellar 1
John M. Floyd

Merry Christmas, James — Wherever You Are! 9
Bill Clark

Silver Dollar Day 13
Averyell A. Kessler

"Hard Candy Christmas" 17
Gail Bouldin

I Remember 19
Dot Day

A Different Christmas Tale 23
Dr. Bob Rich

Paddy's Story 29
Dr. Bob Rich

An Act Of Selfless Love 31
James Davis

You Can't Make It On Your Own 35
Rita F. Purser

Congratulations, You Won! — The Prize Patrol 37
Jas Clark

Heather's Miracle 41
Dot Barker and Heather Bouchillon

Deep Roots 47
Averyell A. Kessler

Singing Of Self 51
Dot Day

Power To Choose 55
Lauren Harris

Wait A Little Longer 57
Jas Clark

Spring Nonsense 59
Dot Day

Spiritual Heart Condition 61
Carl Merchant

Seven Years Out 71
Janet Taylor-Perry

~~**Cinquain**~~**: Sensory Poems** 75
Hazel R. James Lonie

Motivational Analysis: Dorothy Day 81
Madalyn Sheridan Clark

What's Your Favorite Cup Of Tea? 89
Jas Clark

My Grandmother's Love 91
Caryl Hackler

Mission Accepted 93
Larry McAlpin

Big Heart 97
Dot A. Day

Big Heart, Too 103
Dot Day

Addendum, Big Heart 107
Bill Clark, Edited by Barbara Gaddy

Ezekiel Saw The Wheel 119
Averyell Kessler

Behind The Garage 123
Averyell Kessler

Fall #47 125
Dot A. Day

Narrative 129
Lauren E. Harris

Love Of The Game 133
Dot Day

Lula's Memories Of Childhood 135
Dot Barker

The Dress 139
Dot Ainsworth Day

Sleep, Blessed Sleep — Fear Not: He Is With Us! 143
Dot Day

Grandma's Quilts 147
Gail Shows Bouldin

Patterns 149
Gail Shows Bouldin

"I Choose Us" 151
Dot Day

Beyond Belief? 157
Carl Heard

The Tin Whistle 159
Dot Day

Grandpa And Trixie 165
Gail Shows Bouldin

End Of August 167
Ashley Chisholm

Playing Church 175
Dot Day

Dispatch Medic 1! We Need You 10-8 179
Josh Dawson

Love 183
Cindy Mount

Illusion! Epiphany! Proclamation! 187
Janet Taylor-Perry

Fear Not 191
Averyell A. Kessler

Christmas Gift 193
Lottie Brent Boggan

Tippy Toe Dreams 197
Lottie Boggan Brent

Live Sent 201
Courtney Harris

Dear Courtney 203
Dot Day

Layers Of A Painted Life 207
Janet Taylor-Perry

A Dog Moves In 211
Dot Day

How My Dog Saved My Sanity: Or the Benefits of Dog
Ownership on Situationally Depressed Me 215
Dot Day

Therapy Lady 221
Dot Day

Stomach Staples And A Cyclone! 223
Janet Taylor-Perry

Tele-Phony 227
Dot Ainsworth Day

Hagar 231
Janet W. Ferguson

Next Breath, Heaven 233
Dot Day

The Musings of Pauline 241
Pauline Rule
- Introduction 241
- "I Am Come" 243
- "I Am Willing" 248
- "I Am Able" 251
- "I Am There" 253
- "Who Do They Say That I Am?" 262

"Are You the Angel?" 267
Josh Dawson

What's in Your Hand? 273
Dot Day

DELLA'S CELLAR
John M. Floyd

"Oh, no," Billy whispered. He was standing in the tall grass at the top of the hill, his cane fishing pole in one hand and his baseball cap in the other, staring wide-eyed across the fields at the white wooden buildings of the Bloodworth farm. The problem was, the farm didn't look quite the same as it had five hours ago, when he and Jack McClellan had climbed this same hill, heading the other direction.

The reason was simple: the barn was gone.

Billy Kendrix felt sweat break out on his forehead. A chill rippled its way down his spine.

This can't be happening, he thought.

In fact, the barn was not completely gone — some of its blackened framework was still intact, charred and smoldering under the overcast sky. As he watched, too far away to hear anything, a roof beam cracked and toppled into the ashes.

Billy's mouth had gone dry as sandpaper. Dazedly he let his cap and fishing pole drop to the ground. On legs that felt like chunks of stove wood, he began to walk down the long hill toward the farm.

At two hundred yards he could smell the smoke; at a hundred he emerged from a clump of woods and saw Della Bloodworth sitting in a wooden swing near the back steps of the house, staring at the barn with her hands in her lap. Moments later she saw him approaching and walked out to meet him, smoothing her apron. Though he was only twelve years old and she didn't know him from Adam, she greeted him as solemnly as if he were the family minister.

"We've had a bit of excitement, I'm afraid," she said. Then, as she noticed his clothes: "Heavens, child. You're soaking wet."

Billy didn't know how to respond to that. He was used to getting rained on now and then, during his wanderings. And the sudden shower that had caught him and Jack as they fished in Widow Lacey's pond an hour ago had obviously come through here too — water stood in the corn rows, and the rutted driveway was dotted with puddles. Just as obviously, it had come too late to be of any help to the barn.

Looking again at the charred remains, Billy spotted the man he had come to see. Amos Bloodworth, dressed in a straw hat and flannel shirt and overalls, was standing with his back to them, thirty yards away. He appeared to be studying the damage. But it was something else, something in the rain-damp grass only a few feet from the old farmer's work boots that caught Billy's attention.

It was a square pine door, mounted on iron hinges and set flat into the ground some twenty feet from the barn's nearest wall. Under that door, Billy knew, was the wood-bordered entrance to the storm cellar that tunneled underneath the barn.

Trembling now, Billy forced his gaze away from the trapdoor and focused on Mrs. Bloodworth. With a mighty effort he asked, even though he felt sure he already knew the answer, "What happened?"

The old woman sighed. "It started in the storm cellar. This morning, around six."

Billy closed his eyes. His heart sank. He had hoped against hope that maybe, just maybe, his suspicions weren't true. But now he knew.

He opened his eyes to find the old lady staring at him. "I have to talk to Mr. Bloodworth," he said.

She studied him a moment, then turned and walked the short distance to where her husband was standing. Billy saw her speak to him, saw Amos Bloodworth look in his direction. And the weary, frustrated expression on the old man's face — coupled with the fearsome scowl Billy had heard so much about — almost made Billy lose his resolve. Somehow he kept his gaze level and his back straight as Amos looked him over.

The old man didn't come at once, though. He and his wife exchanged several more words, then he handed her something that she examined and tucked into the pocket of her apron. Finally they walked back to where Billy stood waiting.

"You got something to say to me?" Bloodworth asked.

Billy clasped both hands behind his back to keep them from shaking. "Yes, sir. I do."

Amos Bloodworth was quiet a moment, his eyes narrowed. "What's your name?" he said.

"Billy Kendrix."

"You're Will Kendrix's boy?"

When Billy nodded, the old man's face darkened.

"I'm not sure you're welcome here," he said, in a cold voice. "But since you're here anyway, you can tell your daddy I won't have time to listen to any more talk about water rights for his stock. Looks like I'll have my hands full, for a spell. Understand?"

"Yessir."

A silence passed. Amos Bloodworth looked him up and down. "Well? If you have something to tell me, spit it out."

Billy swallowed. "I started the fire," he said.

The old man blinked. "What?"

"It was me," Billy said miserably. "I burned your barn down."

Amos and his wife exchanged a glance. At last he said, "I think you better explain that."

Billy swallowed again, hard. Tears had begun to well up in his eyes. "Jack McClellan and me walked through your woods this morning, a little before six o'clock, on the way to Miz Lacey's pond. When we passed the edge of your yard, we saw the trapdoor to your cellar. Jack ... well, he dared me to go inside. He knew how scared I was of you, and how much you and my daddy don't like each other ..." Billy paused, searching for the right words. "Anyway, he dared me, and I went in."

At that point, Billy happened to glance at Della Bloodworth, who looked almost as if she understood. She had undoubtedly heard the local talk about her and her mysterious husband. Probably because they were childless and kept to themselves, and possibly because of their strange last name, rumor had it that she was a witch and he a warlock, and that their unusual little hole in the ground was the site for all kinds of horrors, not excluding an occasional human sacrifice. In reality, of course, the tunnel was no more than a bomb shelter turned storm cellar turned storeroom — Billy knew that now — but to the local teen and preteen population, "Della's Cellar," as it had come to be called, was haunted.

"You went into our storm cellar?" Amos said, interrupting his thoughts.

Billy's shoulders sagged. "Yes, sir."

The old man regarded him, frowning. "How'd you get in? Through the hole in the barn floor?"

"Through the trapdoor, in the yard."

Amos and his wife exchanged another look. "That end of the tunnel — the trapdoor — was locked," he said.

Billy shook his head. "No, sir. It wasn't. I wish now that it had been."

"But I was down there myself, last week. I pushed up on it from inside. It wouldn't give an inch."

"From inside, it wouldn't have," Billy agreed. "There was a padlock in the ring, holding the doorlatch shut, but it wasn't all the way locked. I just took it off the ring and opened the latch and pulled open the door."

The old man seemed to think that over. "And then?"

"Jack and me went inside."

"How far inside?"

"Only a few steps. Six feet, maybe."

"And how did you see in the dark?"

"I had a book of matches." Billy's face reddened, and again he felt hot tears in his eyes. "I struck one to look around. Then we thought we heard something and left." He paused. "I was sure the match was out …"

Amos Bloodworth stayed silent for several seconds, then cleared his throat. "Let me get this straight. You broke into our storm cellar —"

"It wasn't actually locked, Mr. Bloodworth."

"But you did remove the lock, and open the trapdoor, and go in to snoop around. Right?"

A single tear rolled down Billy's cheek. "Yes, sir."

"What then?"

Billy drew a long, ragged breath and let it out. "Like I said, we thought we heard something farther back in the tunnel toward the barn. We got scared and climbed out. I let the door fall shut after us, but I couldn't find the padlock. It must be over there somewhere —"

"And then you ran away."

"Yessir."

The old man nodded, a stern look on his face. "And where is young McClellan, right now?"

"I don't know," Billy said. "After we got done fishing, he went home through town, to pick up some things for his mama. He wouldn't know yet about the fire."

For a full minute no one said a word. A damp breeze swept in from the hills to the west. A horsefly buzzed past. Somewhere far away, a dog barked.

Amos tucked both hands into the pockets of his overalls and looked Billy in the eye.

"Why did you tell me this?"

The question caught Billy by surprise. "Sir?"

"Nobody saw you here. I would never have known. Ain't that right?"

"I guess so."

"So why did you tell me?"

Billy pondered that for a moment. "I don't know," he said. "I guess … I guess I know it's what my dad would have done."

A long silence passed. Amos studied the boy carefully, then turned and looked at the skeleton of the barn and then past it at the green fields that stretched away to the little creek and the town beyond. Watching the old man stare off into the distance, Billy felt about as guilty as a person could feel, and as sad as he had ever been in his short life.

Finally Amos Bloodworth turned to face him.

"Now I have something to tell <u>you</u>," he said. He took off his straw hat and knelt in the grass at Billy's feet. From a distance of eighteen inches or so, man and boy stared directly into each other's eyes.

"You didn't start the fire," Amos said.

Billy blinked. After a stunned pause he murmured, "But Mrs. Bloodworth told me —"

"That it started in the cellar? It did. But farther in, under the barn. The cat knocked over a lantern."

"The cat?" Billy felt a wave of relief rush through his body. He put out a hand to steady himself, and the old man gently took it in his own.

Holding Billy's small hand, Amos said, "It's a brave thing you did, a brave and noble thing, telling me this. Do you realize that?"

Billy tried to answer, but couldn't. His mind was whirling.

"I admire courage, Billy Kendrix. And honesty." The old man rose to his feet, put his hat on, and looked down at the boy. "I'd be pleased, in a week or so, if you'd come be our guest for supper," he said.

Billy just stared up at him.

"The missus makes a fine meatloaf," Amos added.

Another silence. Billy was vaguely aware that the sun had come out and was warm on his shoulders.

"I'll take that as a yes," Amos said. He started to leave, then stopped and turned again to the young man. "Tell your daddy we'd be pleased to have him and your mother, too."

Then he walked away.

Billy gazed after him with wide eyes. At last he looked at Mrs. Bloodworth, who was still standing there, smiling.

"I don't understand," Billy said.

"You heard him. You earned his respect, for what you did. And for what your folks taught you."

"But what I did was ... I did wrong, and then told the truth about it. That's all."

"No," she said. "That's actually not all." Della Bloodworth's face crumpled and huge tears rolled down her cheeks. In one smooth motion she knelt the way her husband had done and swept the astonished boy into her arms, squeezing him so tight he could hardly breathe.

"What ..." he croaked. "What is it?"

Finally she released him, but remained kneeling at his eye level, holding him with one hand on each shoulder. She was still sniffling.

"How do you suppose the cat knocked over the lantern, child?" she asked. "What do you think a lit lantern was doing down there in the first place?"

"I don't know —"

"It was there because <u>he</u> was there. My Amos had gone down into that cellar this morning, down the stairs inside the barn, to look for me some mason jars. Around six o'clock. That must have been the noise you and your friend heard."

She paused, the tears bright on her pale cheeks.

"What you didn't hear came later," she continued. "Amos said the cat had followed him and knocked the lantern off the peg where he hung it, and some old sacks caught fire." The old woman stopped to wipe her eyes, then touched her palm to his cheek.

"But the sacks — and the fire — were between my Amos and the stairs. He was trapped in the tunnel. He was suffocating there, while I sat in the kitchen, not suspecting a thing. The first I knew was when I saw him walking up the path to the house a while later, his face all smudged and his clothes smoking and the barn burning in the distance." She paused again. "He came very close to dying, down there in that cellar. And he would have, if not for you."

Billy just stared at her. Her blue eyes sparkled through the tears.

"What do you mean?" he asked, his voice hushed.

Without looking down, she reached into her apron pocket and took out the object Amos had handed her. It was an open padlock, still wet from the grass.

"Something sent you here, Billy Kendrix," she said, still smiling. "How could you <u>not</u> be welcome?"

MERRY CHRISTMAS, JAMES — WHEREVER YOU ARE!

Bill Clark

It was Christmas Eve of 1973 when Jean and I took our then two-and-a-half-year-old daughter, Christi Clark Gardner, now grown, to see the decorations and Christmas story as told in multiple displays in a downtown Jackson building, McRae's Department Store. Christi was awestruck! Her parents were, too.

Leaving McRae's that day and driving toward I-55, I took a right turn onto South Jefferson Street toward WLBT where I hung my employment hat back then. "What's up?" Jean asked. I explained that I wanted to check on a buddy of mine who lived next door to the station — a little five-year-old black kid who had become a best friend.

I had somewhat introduced myself by tapping my car horn and waving as I would pass the little house in a row of little houses on the way to the station. One day he ran lickety-split to the parking lot and waited on me to get out of my car, a monstrosity of a vehicle Frank Hutton Lincoln-Mercury furnished me as partial compensation for being their television commercial spokesman. I was riding deep in a Lincoln Continental, and James surely thought I was rich.

"Hi, my name is Bill, what's yours?"

"J A M E S", he replied — in a drawl slow as molasses. Instantly James HAD me!

After that intro it became rather routine that James would run to the parking lot to open my door after I drove past his house. His friendship didn't go unrewarded as he would escort me to the entrance of the station. Over time a piggy bank of change changed hands. If I didn't bring it up, James had a cunning way of dropping hints. Unbeknownst to him, I became a student of his "ways."

On this Christmas Eve, however, I knew I must stop by to check on him. I walked up to the porch where an older brother, perhaps twelve, was sitting in a dilapidated ladder-back chair turned backwards, him blankly staring across the street.

"Is James home?" I inquired.

"James," he yelled out. "You have a visitor." James cracked the door curious as to the visitor and immediately broke out in his killer smile.

"What's Santa bringing tonight?" I asked.

"A bicycle," James responded quite optimistically.

The older brother shook his head to the contrary — unaware that James's friend, then in his early thirties, had gotten to know Santa rather well over the years.

In rather short order, kids began showing up on the porch seemingly from out of the woodwork. Kids I hadn't previously noticed — thirteen in all including those from adjacent houses.

I excused myself and walked to the big 'ol Lincoln where Jean and Christi were watching intently. I asked Jean to get pen and paper; we had work to do. She thought I was CRAZY — and she was right! However, what transpired over the next few hours took on a story book life of its own.

Around 11 p.m., with Mom's gleeful approval, Santa and friends arrived back at James's house with several sleighs — a pickup truck, a station wagon, and two/three cars — loaded with toys and such enough for 13 kids and then some, including a brand-new bike for James fresh off the floor from the Playpen on I-55 North. Dolls, toys of all description, games, clothes, shoes, eats galore and even more bikes ... plus some cash for Mom. You name it — it was on the sleigh. A visit from Santa for the ages! Giggles, laughter, and outright screams rattled what windows were left in the place.

A few months later, James didn't show up for a few days to open my door. Neighbors said they had moved, and none of them seemed to know where. I thought surely James would use one of the toy phones to make contact, but it never happened. However, he did leave a cherished memory that is as vivid today as it was almost 50 years ago.

To this day I am still in awe of those who helped Santa pull off a Christmas miracle on South Jefferson Street for thirteen precious little boys and girls.

Without fail as Christmas nears, James is always in my thoughts, and I think "Merry Christmas, James — wherever you are!"

James would be in his mid-fifties now and I sometime mull sitting down with him over a cup of cider to reflect on that night. I pray he has had a good life and is okay.

Special thanks to: my sister and her husband, James and Martha Carr, my parents Kimble and Margaret Clark, friends Pat and Chuck Miner, Walter and Ann Davis, and Sonny Beckham. Thank you, Don Mizeal, owner of The Playpen, as well, and perhaps others I have forgotten.

Did I mention that Jean was great-with-child? Kim Clark Smith was born five days later on December 29, just in time for a tax deduction. I'm pleased to say that daughters Christi, Kim, and Julie each possess a spirit of looking out for the Jameses (human and animal) who cross their life paths. Julie's passion is doggie rescue.

SILVER DOLLAR DAY
Averyell A. Kessler

For me, the Fourth of July is a silver-dollar day.
My grandfather, WG Avery, started this tradition and it goes way back. When he opened his business in Jackson, he celebrated the Fourth by giving each of his employees a silver dollar for good luck.

He did not reveal that he needed good luck more than most. He'd lost two businesses during the depression, one from fire, the second from a vicious tornado. Mississippi was his last chance to make a go of it. Thankfully, our state was hungry for industry and welcomed him with enthusiasm.

WG knew the ropes of manufacturing having learned the art of the assembly line from Henry Ford, a master teacher in Detroit. Mississippi possessed timber and men seeking jobs in the automobile industry. It was a good match.

After the first tenuous year, his business took off like a downhill locomotive, and he added a second silver dollar to the good luck pot. The next year three, then four. He was up to seventeen when I joined him for the silver dollar ceremony. Late on the afternoon of July 3, he blew the quitting time whistle and gathered his men on a loading dock fronting on the Illinois Central's Mill Street train track. The day was blisteringly hot, but no one noticed.

Dorothy A. Day

My grandfather gave the same speech every year. "No work tomorrow. It's the Fourth of July! My men need spending money in their pockets and a new shirt on their backs." In today's money, seventeen dollars equals about $160.00. Behind him were envelopes of silver dollars and stacks of shirts, all large or extra-large. No one wanted a medium or a small, and if they did, they wouldn't admit it.

I watched as each man's name was called and he stepped forward to shake hands with WG and pick a shirt. Once done, my grandfather ripped open a money envelope and poured a shower of silver dollars into his hands. I stood beside him as it happened again and again, until all 103 men had a new shirt and celebration money. When it was over and the men drifted away, he handed me a silver dollar and said "Remember, girl, you can do anything you want to do."

It was a casual comment, tossed off like a high pop fly straight into center field. An odd one also. He was a 19th century man, born, reared and working long before women had the right to vote. I was a shy nine-year-old still negotiating my way through the intricacies of Power School, diving lessons, pesky neighborhood boys, and the perils of being an only child. At first, I didn't understand. Me? Anything? Unusual advice for a young female in the 1950s South. Not the traditional life plan offered up during those years. But his words stuck with me, and I still think about them.

I don't focus on "you can do anything," because I certainly won't be a coloratura soprano, a hot shot investment advisor or win an Olympic gold medal. I listen to the words "anything you want to do." I call it chasing dreams. The Declaration of Independence calls it the pursuit of happiness.

Independent thought and authentic dreams are a rare commodity these days, especially in a cut-and-paste society. If thoughts are clear and dreams are strong, they'll blaze like a torch in the midnight sky. That's the gift of July Fourth. The right to dream,

Ordinary Miracles

imagine, try, fail, and try again. Dreams are the basis of all creative endeavor. Age is not a diminishing factor; neither is youth. The pursuit of happiness is an unalienable right, and just as important as the right to life and liberty. What a blessing!

WG continued his silver dollar event adding one each year until his bank complained about locating so many silver dollars. All the fun dribbled away when he handed out cash instead of a sparkling handful of silver. But he kept at it. Shirts, too.

I've still got my silver dollar. It's called a Morgan dollar and features a radiant lady liberty and the words E Pluribus Unum. If anyone tries to pry it out of my hands, take care! Lady liberty still rules the day, and we are still out of many, one.

"HARD CANDY CHRISTMAS"
Gail Bouldin

Years ago when I was 12 years old, I lived with my mom and four younger sisters in those apartments on Beacon Street.

My mom and dad had just divorced, and money was tight. It was Christmas time, and we had no money for food, much less a tree or presents. Mama was working at a little cafe and made just enough for rent and utilities. We ate on her tip money. As Christmas drew near, Mom was worried because she knew that it was going to be a sad time for her kids with not even being able to get a tree.

Three young guys that lived close knew the situation, and one of them brought a tree while the other two swiped ornaments and lights from their mom's house and brought them to us. We didn't know this until later. Then, my uncle Jim brought us big boxes of food with everything one could want to eat.

Another man, a customer of mom's, gave me five dollars. All of us kids drew names and we each took a dollar and bought that sister a present. That year we didn't have a lot, but we had a beautiful tree and plenty to eat. Plus, each of us had our sister present to open that Christmas morning. Many Christmases have come and gone since then and certainly were more prosperous, but none as memorable.

I REMEMBER

Dot Day

Saving pennies, nickels, and dimes in a jelly jar
'cause Mike was gonna take us to the state fair
after the cotton was all picked.
Seeing colored horses going up and down,
but so much racket,
and Momma wouldn't find me in all the people,
and I didn't ride.
Walking the board fence at the Buckley house;
it was Thanksgiving 'cause I was eating fruitcake.
Riding in the rumble seat of Joe's "ole Betsy"
all the way to Ethel Turnage's store.
Going to Aunt Ethel's;
Joe telling me to ask Daddy to stop for ice cream
'cause my throat hurt, and he did!
Riding on the crossbar of the trike behind Sonny
(Now I wonder if I ever got to sit on the seat.)
Waiting and waiting for the school bus
and wondering when Sonny could come home.
Having feet in sandals (not in black patent Mary Janes),
dressed in Mama's creation,
going with Lurlene every Sunday to Lone Star Methodist Church

Dorothy A. Day

(but being reminded by her that she always had to walk
because Sonny or I would refuse to ride with whoever offered).
Picking cotton and getting behind
and being fussed at because I was always dreaming.
Waiting again for the bus —
Joe had gone to Mississippi State
Getting hoisted onto his shoulders — me on one side,
Sonny on the other
(What did he do with his clothes and gear?)
and going in probably to feast on teacakes and buttermilk —
Momma always liked to fix the favorites, and those were Joe's.
Playing and singing and learning of love in a place called Bible
School, which was at the church, but outside,
and learning to like the taste of red Kool-Aid.
Hearing the insistent car horn coming around the big curve:
Maxine and Hubert announcing their arrival from New Orleans.
Lying in bed, Sonny on one side, Dot on the other, Lur in the
middle, arms outstretched to hold a child and telling of stories
(She has always sacrificed.)
Relying on big brothers and sisters for Christmas gifts.
(Lur still hurts at the tobacco and snuff bought,
but never enough for Santa Claus from the folks.)
Getting to choose a doll,
a huge stuffed bear from the Sears, Roebuck catalogue
— Joe was far away in the Army in Germany
And Sonny remembers Uncle Pat coming home from Texas
with lots of money, big cars, Stetson hats, presents for Dickie,
Ronnie, Dwight,
but not for Dot and Sonny.
(He was just an old drunk.)
Going swimming with Maxine and Calvie Jean
and bunches of others and being taught
it was better to lie than tell of fun.

Ordinary Miracles

Riding the school bus to Prentiss
and having enough money to choose what I wanted to buy
— *Black Beauty* by Anna Sewell
and discovering it was okay to cry.
Giving my doll to my new niece — Lur's baby girl.
(And she grew enough to cut off my doll's curls!)
Growing enough to discover even moms and dads like kisses as I tucked them in
'cause I had to stay up to study, to work, and to dream.

A DIFFERENT CHRISTMAS TALE

Dr. Bob Rich

He holds the knife a few inches in front of my nose. I can't breathe, just stare into his eyes. A sty on his left eyelid. Coarse black pores on his nose. Gaps among his teeth as he growls, "Whatever cash you got, now!"

A warm wet trickle of urine ran down my left leg, and I hate the tremble in my voice. "I … haven't got any on me, honest."

"Yeah, right! You got a wallet?"

"Not with me. Look … I just went for a walk, and …"

"Yeah, that means you got a home, right?"

"Wh … what do you mean?"

"Look mate, it's the billionaires' Australia, right? I sleep in me car, and with prices through the roof, it's food or petrol." The fierce glare is gone from his eyes.

"Um … can you PLEASE put that knife away?"

He looks puzzled, then gazes at the knife. I think he's actually forgotten about it. He withdraws his hand, folds the knife, and pockets it.

Time starts moving. We live again.

"Then I toddled along. Old bloke, easy mark, right?" Might as well copy his speech; it could relax him a little. "I am sorry for your troubles, but it's not my doing."

His shoulders were now hunched. With my panic gone, I could see him as a person: a weedy little fellow in shabby clothes, but, surprisingly, clean-shaven. Twenty years ago, I could have overpowered him, knife or no, but an eighty-one-year-old like I am is not much for fighting anymore.

"Look, mate, sorry. I figured I'll hold up the next person what walks along the path. Either I grab enough for a pizza, or land in jail. Roof over me head, three meals a day, right?"

Once more I could enjoy the scent of freshly-mown grass, hear the whisper of a light breeze in the leaves of the tree he'd hidden behind, appreciate blue sky over green park. "Look." I could now speak calmly. "Come with me to my place, and I'll give you ten dollars as a Christmas present."

Suddenly, he looked beautiful. Oh, his face was still nothing to look at, he was still a near-skeleton in half-rags, but the brown eyes shone at me almost with a light of their own.

"You're amazing, mate. Which way we goin'?"

I turned and he walked beside me, matching my slow pace while saying, "On weekdays, I get food from that church charity mob, but weekends is somethin' else. The hospital is real good; you can have a shower there, and they even give you a free razor and toothbrush when you don't bring your own. I may be a hobo, but don't wanna stink, right?"

"You've got it all worked out, I can see. Oh, my name is Mario Cellini."

"Italian?" He said it "Eye-talyan."

"No. My grandparents were, but I'm true-blue Aussie."

He grinned. "I'm Paddy Murphy."

"Irish?" I asked to get back at him. He laughed with me.

"Genuine convict stock way back. Guess I'm returnin' to the family tradition."

"Those Irish convicts weren't criminals but sort of political prisoners."

"Howd'ya know?" He looked really interested, not merely making conversation.

"I used to be an English, history and geography teacher, and my current project is writing my fourth book on Australian history."

"Well, I never! A scholar!"

We reached my house, and I opened the gate for him. He looked at the long grass, weeds in the flower beds, so I had to explain, "I can't do it anymore and can only afford a garden service once a month."

"You got a mower and a spade? Look, order a pizza for the two of us, and I'll fix your garden."

Wonderful. Barter is much better than charity.

In an hour, all the weeds were in a pile, grass mown and the flower beds mulched with the cuttings, and we were sitting in my kitchen sharing the pizza and cups of tea.

"You live here alone?"

I felt the tears threaten. "Kids, grandkids, and great-grandbabies are interstate. My wife ... passed away ten months and three days ago .... This'll be my first Christmas without her."

"In a way, that's how I ended up on the streets. Lost me wife and kids."

"Oh, I am sorry. Did they ..."

"Die? Nah. I had a good job, train driver, but took amphetamines to stay awake. And that led to more and more, then ice, and, oh hell, I got violent. Court order. Can't see me kids. And lost me job."

We shared a long silence, one of mutual suffering and mutual support. Then he stood.

"Mario, mate, thank you."

"Your work was worth far more than the cost of a pizza."

"Mate, given from the heart both ways, right? Well, I'll be goin'."

Next morning, 9 o'clock, he knocked on my front door. When I opened it, he said, "Sunday, right? Still no charity food, and I noticed cobwebs on your walls and that. Can we do another trade?"

"Come in, Paddy. Yes, the council cleaning lady only has half an hour a week."

So, I provided breakfast; then for about three hours he was a whirlwind around the house. At the end of it, everything shone, and he sprawled on the sofa, hardly able to move. "Ain't used to the exercise, right?" he groaned. "But hey, the results is worth it."

We shared lunch, then I left him in front of the TV — a great luxury to him, he said — and I sat in my office, working on my book. In the evening, I whipped up a spaghetti bolognaise. During the last three years of Agnes's life, while caring for her, I had to do everything, including the cooking.

I got out a bottle of merlot, but Paddy said, "You go ahead mate, but it's the brain poisons what wrecked me life, right? After I came out of rehab, I never touched none. Even got off the smokes, that was the hardest, but hell, who can afford the tax they put on it?"

So, to act with respect, I put the wine away, and having company at dinner once more was such a good change. It's during the normally shared times I'd been missing Agnes the most.

Then the little fellow surprised me. "Mario, mate, listen. I been on the streets three years. And Christmas is the worst day of the year. Me kids might as well be dead. And if I was allowed near them, hell, what'd they think of a homeless bastard what can't afford to give them a present?"

He stopped, head hanging down, obviously holding back the tears. "Look, mate, next Wednesday is Christmas, right? I wanna spare you havin' to go through it alone. Can I come?"

He was right. Heavens, he just had to be right.

On the morning of Christmas day, he was on my doorstep carrying a thick photo album. I'd waited with breakfast for his arrival, and we shared it; then I sat beside him, and we looked through his life.

Train driver in uniform. He was still short of course, but with meat on his bones and a mouthful of teeth, a good-looking youngster. Here he was in control of huge freight trains and packed suburban ones, then at a nightclub with a pretty blonde, about his height. He sang, in a surprisingly pleasant tenor,

Nancy, Nancy,
All so fine and fancy,
Then some day, along the way,
My Nancy's gone away.

"Well, it was me what had to go away, right?" Tears wetted both his face and voice. Wedding photos, the birth and steady growth of two girls and a boy, big family occasions, and through it all, Paddy looking more and more gaunt, the smile on his face forced. Then on the last page, police mugshots, dead eyes staring at the camera.

"Let's go back to the start," I said and had him tell me the good stories from those good times.

Then it was my turn. I have all my photos scanned, so it was on the computer. Me as a little boy, then captain of the school football team, getting my black belt in Aikido, proud graduate. Various girlfriends, then pictures with Agnes, the same clichés of life as in his: wedding, four kids born and growing, kids' weddings, and grandkids ....

A separate folder showed me with all the many classes of children in my charge, speeches at conferences, receiving awards, a long series of me as Principal, retirement.

Then the covers of my three books to date, book launches with silver-haired Agnes proudly beside me.

"There is one more folder," I said, heavily, "the last few years through the cancer."

"Nah," Paddy said. "Stick with the good times, right? Mario, so, Agnes was a science teacher, you said?" We kept chatting late into the night.

Then I had a thought. "Paddy, I'd like to offer you another trade. I can't drive anymore. I've got a spare room. You've got a car."

PADDY'S STORY
Dr. Bob Rich

After I finished *A Different Christmas Tale*, for months I was worried about the future. Mario was old and guaranteed to die sooner or later. But, then, Paddy told me all about it:

'Bout a month ago, Mario sent his book off to the publisher. Funny though, a publisher called Penguin. I mean, that's a bird, right?

And yesterday, we celebrated his eighty-second birthday. Don't know how you do these things, but somehow he used his computer and the telly to have all his family chattin' with us like they was TV stars, 'cept each of his kids and grandkids and families was in a sort of a movie box. But they could see Mario and me, and we could see them, right?

That was yesterday. This morning, he didn't show as usual, so I waited for a while. An old fella like him is allowed to sleep in. But when he still wasn't up at 10 o'clock, I knocked on his door.

No answer. I called out a few times, then opened the door.

He was in bed, where else? But his eyes was open, his mouth was open, and … ohmegod, he wasn't breathing.

First thing I did was cried. I know, big boys don't do that, but hell, he rescued me off the streets, and he and his lawyer son was helpin' me to apply to the court to allow me to see me family again, and anyway, I love the old fella. He even paid for false teeth for me, wouldya believe? Been in his house near enough six months now, and never a cross word between us, right?

No good calling an ambulance. He was way beyond that. But what to do, then?

I managed to get his computer going, and I've seen him get at the phone numbers and things, so found his doctor's number and called that. They know me 'cause I've often driven the old boy to his appointments. So, she says, "Mr. Murphy, leave it with us."

Gladly, but now came a harder call. I found Rosemary's number. That's Mario's oldest and the one what organizes everything. Somehow, I stammered out to her that her dad was gone. We cried together on the phone. Then she said, "Paddy, I'll need to talk it over with the others, but we can probably let you stay on."

That was decent of her, right? I said so. But, the carer's allowance I was on for lookin' after Mario was, like, $900 a fortnight, but goin' back to Jobseeker is $550. And Mario paid for food and fuel for me car, and stuff like that. So, even if the rest of the family agreed, I was still in a bit o' trouble.

And there's council rates, and insurance, and electricity and stuff, so it wasn't fair they couldn't rent it out, and no way could I pay rent like in nearby houses, like $400 a week!

An ambulance-looking thing turned up, and they took poor old Mario's body.

Just for somethin' to do, I made his bed and tidied up, then sat around, me mind a blank, till the phone rang. It was Jeremy, Mario's son from Perth. He's been helpin' us with applying to see me family again, 'cause he is a lawyer. I've never liked lawyers, but Jeremy is straight as a die. Mario's son, right?

And Jeremy said, "Paddy, listen. We got all that documentation that you are completely off addictive substances. We can extend what we're asking for, you with me?"

"Like what?"

"Would you like to drive trains again?"

AN ACT OF SELFLESS LOVE

James Davis

The little bedroom community of D'Lo has been home to my family and me since 1974.

My son grew up here, and I will always consider it home. It's a wonderful place to live, being firmly rooted in a strong love for God and country. Having laid the groundwork as to the solidity of the little town, I'd like to tell the true story of a remarkable man who had served our country during WWII, then returned to D'Lo to live humbly and frugally in the same little house in which he'd grown up. It no longer stands but was located about four blocks from my own.

Cletus was already fairly reclusive and a "town character" by the time I first met him. I found him to be quiet, soft-spoken, shy, and always dressed in overalls and a cap. His house, in a sad state of disrepair, had never been painted and desperately needed shoring up. Little was known publicly of Cletus other than what I've said. He ran, by the time I met him, what was called "The D'Lo Taxi." For a nominal fee, he would simply take people to town for appointments. His life appeared to be one played out by minding his own business and being a law-abiding citizen.

Into this setting, a lady appeared one day in D'Lo, and no one seemed to know much about her, but she was said to be living in the house with Cletus. This was at a time when such wasn't done, especially not in D'Lo. From what we could learn, there was no romantic relationship. Callie Mae was a pretty middle-aged lady, was rarely seen in public, and one could tell by looking at her that she had obviously suffered a reversal of fortune in her life. I only saw her and Cletus riding together in his old truck maybe twice.

Then, late one evening, our town marshal Joe, who was a close friend of mine, called to ask if I'd ride with him around the corner to Cletus's house. Cletus was dead! I did go with Joe to Cletus's house, and we were met at the front door by Callie Mae, who was visibly distraught, though in control. She had been weeping; it was clear. When Joe asked where the body was, Callie Mae pointed to a back bedroom.

While we waited for the coroner, Joe, Callie Mae, and I sat in the little sitting room. At a point in the brief conversation, Joe asked Callie Mae, "How did you end up living with Cletus, Callie Mae?" I thought it a rather forward question, considering the circumstances.

Gathering all the strength and reserve she could muster, Callie Mae stated very clearly and succinctly to us both, "When I had no place else to go, Cletus took me in." That statement told me all I needed to know about Cletus and Callie Mae. I, really for the first time, saw Cletus as a giant of a man who saw a need and reached out in compassion and met it. In so doing, he saved a lady who was desperate at a point in her life and allowed her to keep her dignity. I came away from that house on that fateful night thanking God for Cletus while praying for Callie Mae and whatever the future might hold for her.

As I've said, this story played out in the 1970s. I could never learn what happened to Callie Mae after Cletus's death. She simply disappeared, and, with no heirs, Cletus's acre or two were sold, and the little house was soon torn down. Two lives intersected four blocks from me, and I am still saddened that I thought myself too busy to take the time to get to know them both. It has been one of my greatest regrets.

YOU CAN'T MAKE IT ON YOUR OWN
Rita F. Purser

DC Yearwood said he learned long ago that people have to help other people.

What a privilege it was for me to have known DC Yearwood through my work at Pyle, Harris, Dreher and Mills, a Jackson law firm in the 1980s. DC was a process server and messenger for the law firm, after working 25 years with the Hinds County Chancery Court system. Our friendship continued for many years and as long as he lived.

"You can't make it on your own," said Mr. Yearwood, who went out of his way to help out since the days of the Great Depression in Sicily Island, Louisiana, until he passed.

"When I was fifteen, a man got me started by giving me a job at his grocery store," Yearwood is reported to have said. A few years later he moved to Little Rock, Arkansas, to be a bus driver. "A German fellow named Hostedtier fed me and gave me a place to stay until I got on my feet."

Known as the "Good Samaritan" of Jackson, Mississippi, DC never passed up an opportunity to help someone in need. He received a tremendous amount of pleasure from helping other people and never expected or wanted anything in return.

He would frequently stop to help a stranded motorist or escort a visitor to town to his/her destination. I remember one occasion when a woman was in Jackson to deliver some legal papers to a family. DC not only led her to the home but waited while she finished her business and helped her find her way out of town.

I remember another occasion when DC saw a young woman hitchhiking with her two children and he stopped and gave them a ride. He and his wife, Vera, took them into their home for a period of time until a family member of the mother was able to help them.

It would not be unusual for DC to be late getting back to the law firm from an errand because he had stopped to lend someone a helping hand.

DC's good works inspired many others. Vera started a thrift shop in her church to help people in need. One of DC and Vera's daughters, Jackie, inspired by both her parents, started a blanket ministry in her church and more than 10,000 people received a comfort blanket from that ministry.

Needless to say, I will never forget DC Yearwood and the impact he had on my life. I thank God for having known him. His example inspired everyone who knew him to do more for others.

CONGRATULATIONS, YOU WON! — THE PRIZE PATROL

Jas Clark

As I am looking out this window of life this morning, I am remembering how much money my mama sent in to the Reader's Digest to win the big prize money, and waiting for the Prize Patrol to show up with money that lasts for a lifetime.

She didn't do it for herself, but to make sure her family would be taken care of after she was gone and not have to struggle. I told her, "I've been struggling all my life, it's all right. Granny told me the Lord will see us through." Mama, bless her heart, wanted better for us, so she kept trying. I knew time was running out — her Alzheimer's was defeating me. It was taking one thing after another from her whole body, but mostly her mind. It was the hardest thing I ever went through.

The Prize Patrol commercial came on television, and she told me, "I'm going to win that one day. We won't have to worry about a thing."

I decided I had to find a way to let her "win." I got a sweet couple to come to my house and pretend they were the Prize Patrol. I got roses, balloons, made the sign to go on the vehicle, and made the huge check. On that day, I met the sweet couple down the road, put the sign on the car, and gave them the check, roses, and balloons and then waited for them to arrive. Some family came to help set this up with me and witness it. I thought it would be the best gift in the world, and the best thing I could ever give her — finally to win the Prize Patrol.

They knocked on our door, and I asked Mama, "I wonder who that is."

She said, "It's no telling. Go see."

I opened the door and the man at the door said, "I'm looking for Mrs. Eva Nell Berry."

I said, "Mama, a nice-looking man wants to see you."

She got up and looked at him and saw the flowers, balloons, and that big check and I yelled with excitement, "Oh, my sweet Mama, you have won!!!"

She asked, "What?"

I said, "You finally won the Prize Patrol like on TV." The smile on her face was priceless — she was so excited, just couldn't believe it.

She was so thrilled. It was the best day of her life. We counted her out a thousand dollars, and she thought she was in Heaven. She was so happy, and she wouldn't let anyone touch that big display check I made her, either! She held onto it for dear life.

Everyone left and she said, "Baby, you can have all this money."

I teared up and told her, "You are going to spend every last dime of this on whatever you want." Her face and her excitement made her remember me that day, if only for a few seconds. The couple was so sweet to do this for her. I thank them from the bottom of my heart. I thank everyone that came to share in one of the happiest days of my mama's life.

She was my Winner as a mama. I may never be able to top making anyone as happy as I made her that day. I've done so much

Ordinary Miracles

wrong in my life; but I believe the Lord will forgive me for staging all of that for my mama. He knows I'm a sinner trying to do better.

Note to the Prize Patrol: We couldn't wait any longer ….

Proverbs 23:25 "Thy father and thy mother shall be glad, and she that bare thee shall rejoice."

HEATHER'S MIRACLE
Dot Barker and Heather Bouchillon

The young woman walked into the room with her black eyes shining asking, "Want to see my painting?"

I assured her I would love to see the box of paintings she was carrying. As I began to look at each picture, the smiling face of the young lady disappeared into another time.

It was a lazy day in September 1993, when the telephone broke the silence of the afternoon. My sister-in-law, Lena, in a distressed voice pleaded, "Please go to the hospital and be with Heather. She has been in an accident, and she may not make it. We are bringing her from Louisville by helicopter, and no one will be there." Almost in shock, I promised her my husband James and I would be at the hospital when Heather arrived.

Heather was my brother's oldest grandchild and very dear to his wife, Lena. My brother, Merle, died when Heather was two years old. She was now sixteen and just got her driver's license.

James and I arrived at the hospital and waited for Janie and Mike, Heather's parents, to arrive. The pastor of their church was driving them from Louisville to Baptist Hospital. When they arrived, Dr. Neill, the neurologist, called the family into a conference room to talk about Heather's condition. The news was not good, but she would live. Jenny was holding Heather's stuffed bear in her arms. As she heard the words, "She will live," the tears flowed as she rocked back and forth squeezing the bear.

The reality set in as the doctor's words began about the traumatic brain injury. Heather had a severed left optic nerve. The brain was swelling, and this had to be brought under control before there was more damage to the brain. The next 72 hours were critical. We should be cautiously optimistic about the amount of recovery.

While in ICU Heather had a stroke which left her partly paralyzed on the right side. Dr. Neill informed the parents that their daughter would never walk or talk.

The prayers began immediately as the story of Heather's accident was spread from Louisville throughout the state of Mississippi and parts of Arkansas.

As my husband and I made our weekly visits to the hospital, the story of Heather's accident and how it happened came to light. Heather was driving to a friend's house when the rain started, and the inexperienced driver lost control of the car. The brakes locked as she rounded the curve, and she hit an electric pole.

Mr. Livingston, checking on the electric outage, came upon the wrecked car at the electric pole. He found Heather in the car, drowning in her own fluids. This man was the first miracle in Heather's life.

A highway patrolman was called to the scene, and the parents were called about the accident. The parents, along with Mike's two brothers, arrived at the accident. Heather's mother, Janie, was kept from the car because at that moment the officer on the scene thought the girl in the car had died. As Janie stood grieving, a crowd had gathered; from the crowd a woman emerged and asked if she could pray with her. Through her tears. Janie told her, "Please do, because right now my heart is breaking." The identity of the woman was never known, but she was seen at the funeral of a student killed in a car accident the same week of Heather's accident.

Concerned citizen or an angel from God?

The ambulance carried Heather to the local hospital. The doctor on duty called for a medevac helicopter to come for her. The helicopter couldn't fly in the rain, so the local ambulance had to make the long run to Baptist Hospital in Jackson. No family member could ride to Jackson in the ambulance because the medical team in the ambulance was trying to keep Heather alive.

Janie and Mike stayed at the hospital day and night for the first ten days. Lena, the grandmother, was staying with their younger daughter Stefanie while the parents were waiting outside the ICU.

Janie had just started a new teaching position at the beginning of the new school year. She had to return to work to keep her job and insurance.

Week after week, Heather lay in the hospital bed with her eyes open, never showing any sign of recognizing anyone. She had been placed in a room in the Restorative Care Unit after two weeks in the ICU. A family member could have a place to stay and be with their beloved child. Lena was then staying with Heather during the week so her parents could return to their respective jobs. Each Wednesday, Mike, Janie, and Stefanie would come to the hospital. The parents would come down and stay the weekend while the grandmother went home.

One side of Heather's beautiful long black hair had been shaved from her head for surgery, so Janie had someone cut the other side very short. Someone at that time believed he noticed a tear on Heather's cheek.

On January 2, 1994, Heather was allowed to go home in a coma with a blood clot on her brain. This clot could have caused instant death. Over a period of several months and many prayers the blood clot dissolved.

The first day home Heather began to wake up and know that she was home, but she still could not talk. Each piece of furniture had a name, and she was retrained as one would a newborn. Dr. Neill had cautioned the family that when Heather awoke, and if she ever talked again, she would be either very humble or very aggressive. The family worked daily, tenderly caring for Heather, and soon her strength began to return.

One day she burped and giggled. Janie said, "Heather, if you can giggle, you can talk. Say 'Mama.'"

She repeated, "Mama."

Janie told her to say, "Thank you, Jesus." Again, Heather repeated her mother's words. After much rejoicing by the family, word began to spread.

Next, Heather wanted to call Dr. Neill. After he heard Heather's voice, he informed the family that he had just witnessed a miracle. God wasn't through with Heather because another prayer had been answered. Heather was very humble and spoke only with love for her family and friends.

With speech, occupational and physical therapy at home, Heather showed improvement to amaze everyone. A brace was placed on her right leg to help her on the long road to walking again.

Heather was carried to Methodist Rehab in Jackson. They asked what her goal would be with treatment. She had been chosen to be a member of the color guard for the band. She wanted to be able to walk down the hall and twirl her flag. She did, and the staff again said they had seen a miracle.

In August Heather went back to school, and with the help of Mrs. Jewell relearned most of the skills that had been lost with the traumatic brain injury. When asked to write an essay of what she planned to do in school, Heather's essay was very simple." I want to be able to walk without assistance and receive my high school diploma. I know all things are possible through God."

A pastor from a local church wrote the weekly newsletter and I quote his reflections: "Every so often mere mortals have the privilege of seeing the face of God etched within the framework of rather ordinary events of life. I had one of those moments attending the graduation exercises at Louisville High School.

"It was a nice graduation, and if one was not paying attention, you might have missed the moment. The name Heather Bouchillon rang out and reverberated back from the red clay hillsides of the town. A young woman slowly climbed the steps and approached the school officials who waited to present her with her high school diploma.

"I had visited Heather and noticed the frail body of the girl with the determined look in her eyes as I asked her what her goals might be for herself. 'First, I intend to graduate from high school.' There were tears of joy over Heather reaching her goal. Heather, we are also proud of you and thank God for allowing us to share in your miracle."

"Aunt Dot, you want one of the pictures I painted?" asked Heather as I was brought back to the young woman with the box of paintings. "Some are abstract," she added.

"That means she doesn't know what they are or what she was painting," laughed the proud grandmother, Lena.

I proudly display two of these pictures painted by a walking miracle named Heather.

DEEP ROOTS
Averyell A. Kessler

Ralph Waldo Emerson: "Earth laughs in flowers."

What an interesting thought. Especially now when laughter is rare, but flowers are not. April brings them on, as she always does, chasing winter away and filling her arms with daffodils, roses, and four o'clocks with bright faces. She smiles and waves as azaleas open and a clematis vine winds its way around my fence post. When May arrives, there's no holding back. Three ancient magnolias will bloom in my front yard showing off velvet petals and sending out the sweetest perfume this side of the Mississippi. Outside, on my patio, a tiny begonia I considered a goner is returning to life, and tiny green shoots are emerging from a left-for-dead poinsettia. They survived with deep roots.

I grew up in a world overflowing with plants and flowers. That's not unusual in the South. My father was a happy gardener, if not a skilled one. Every year he tended a small triangular plot of Dutch Iris by the side of our house, blessing them with Vigoro until lovely purple blossoms appeared. He also planted a row of red floribunda roses but removed them when I tripped over a jump rope, fell into a cluster of thorns, and howled like a hyena. His grape vine experiment went well for a while, until he realized that it was a friend of

Godzilla's and the vine overtook Mama's clothesline. Not a single grape appeared, so he stuck to Big Boy tomatoes for the next few years. Finally, he decided he'd limit his gardening activities to raking leaves and mowing the grass. A good decision.

My grandfather WG was also a flower guy. As soon as he was able, he purchased thirty acres of raw land on County Line Road and trucked up a load of azaleas and camellias from the Gulf Coast. He fashioned a loosely organized garden, no landscapers allowed. Later he dug a well and laid down pipes to draw water from his ponds. Fertilizer came from a highly suspicious source and smelled worse than rotten eggs. One rule prevailed. Never, under any circumstances, cut down a tree. Especially his single prized sycamore which made a mess and dropped spikey brown balls every spring. To him, each tree was sacrosanct as well as his best friend. The house he built in Avery Gardens was constructed without sacrificing a single tree. Ours, on the far side of the pond, caused the loss of only two.

"What's wrong with cutting down a tree?" I asked him.

"There's no life without trees," he answered. "No oxygen. No rain either." Tenth grade biology was still miles away and I was amazed by this news.

"Trees are meant to last," he continued. "It's almost impossible to dig one up because they have deep roots."

I've been thinking about deep roots lately, especially since we're living in a scenario that seems to be taken from the book of Job. During the last few months, my small, poor state has been overtaken by floods, unrelenting rain pocked with deadly tornadoes and straight-line winds strong enough to topple whatever stands in the way. Hurricane season is closing in, and no one knows what that will bring. Now the shadowy specter of disease has inched its way into everyday life, spreading its boney fingers and gobbling up any semblance of normality.

Ordinary Miracles

For the past few weeks, television commentators and various government officials have assured us that we're going to get through this. That somehow, we'll stumble along in this "new normal," adapt to it and survive our fate. I disagree. In my small conundrum of a state, we may be down, but not out. We're scared, but we're strong. If we fall on our knees, it's for prayer, not begging. We'll win out in the end because of grit and determination.

Grace, courage and fortitude have been hiding for a long time. Finally, they've emerged, with flags flying and a big brass band. Quite simply, we want life back, our life. That's a demand, not a request. When the storms die away, we'll fight hard to rebuild shattered lives, and houses too. As flood waters recede, we'll pull strength from the wreckage, mop up and start again.

Medicine has beaten polio, smallpox and measles, as well as whooping cough, tetanus, mumps and rubella. It will beat the virus too. That's a statement, not a guess. Like the ancient magnolias growing outside my windows, our roots are deep. They are wide, permanent and secure enough to anchor us to the earth and to each other. They are strong enough to bind up hurt and turn trouble back on its heels. We will prevail because our roots are deep, as is our faith and family. We are meant to last. So, April, bless us with an abundance of flowers. We need them right now.

SINGING OF SELF
Dot Day

I have filled my life with frivolity;
I have been entertained.
Feast, fast, ball game of life …
Gone my chance for glory; but then, who's to blame?
My life was spent in pleasure —
Reckless, heedless, dissolute, caring not at all.
Going my way, pleasure my thought —
Forgetting truth and loveliness — now what legacy can remain?

My lesson to me — live and matter — look up and trust:
Live beyond self — joy in the joy given others.
I sit to write, to dream, to let things matter —
And I wonder, "What have I poured in?"
I see the people around me and I despise the choices we let
others make.
I <u>must</u> matter … I <u>must</u> choose … or lose the right of choice.

You chose a simpler way, you boxcar family:
There is food on your table, clothes upon your back.
You bathe less frequently, visit the garbage pail for your snack.
"Neglect," we say and take your child away.

Dorothy A. Day

You chose, but not to suit us.
It must be <u>our</u> way.

I see you, involved one, demanding your way,
Leading and going whether we follow or not
(But blindly and stupidly we do).
You are so sure; there is no doubt.
Did you never taste of uncertainty and know of its gall?

A woman stayed home one day, and at the sink she stood.
Her wonder was of schools and children learning to go —
And the choices others made for them.

I see you, woman at the sink;
You think of old times and old ways
Of a simpler time when all were poor
And it didn't matter.
You hurt and ache at the desire unfulfilled;
But you see the want and the children go.
You wonder at the new world and the new god
And long for the Old.

I see you, little earth mother, loving and caring and prophet
of doom.
Picketing and making a statement but rarely a difference.
The world will die and wonder why.
You will say, "I told you ... I told you of hairspray, of ozone,
of chemicals, of pollution, of germs and bombs,
I told you. I told you."

I see you, working mother, balancer of life's accounts
And nothing is in balance (not your life, your job, your husband,
nor the place where you live).

You juggle the demands: two in the air and one in the hand.
And the waiting whine, "My turn. My turn. MINE!"

I see you, despised one;
You doubt yourself because their envy makes them bold.
You hang your head and wonder
And hate and revenge become your aim.
"Consider the Source."

You chose to be better, you forgiving one.
I think of your betrayal and ponder,
"What would have been my revenge?"
Bitter or better, and you chose the better route.

I look at others, and I see me:
Choosing to observe, seldom to participate,
Sympathizing, near-empathizing
But scared to let you know I see
(And afraid of dividing my time; I, too, must juggle).

I delight in beginnings, sorrow in endings,
confound in middlings, and sit on the fence through it all.
I sing of me, alive and free
Free for the moment in the wonder of it all
But bound
Bound to do and to be the best that I can
(And I wonder, "What if my best is not good enough?" and
"What if I waste my best?")
Bound to the land
Of beginnings and teachings and planting of new crops in ground
grown stale
Needing renewal — Must I compost myself yet again?
I haven't the strength or the will. BURNOUT!

Dorothy A. Day

> Bound to the family and loving my bonds.
> Bound to my Lord,
> And my song no longer is of me.
> My song is of Him who died and lives,
> Of Him who encourages and gives
> Gifts of courage, of comfort and love and peace
> and erasures of doubt,
> And he spends His time explaining me and my ways to God
> And loving me, and loving me, and loving me.
> I sang of Jesus and the song was of love,
> From a child, alone and surrounded
> "Jesus Loves Me," my comfort, my shout.

POWER TO CHOOSE

Lauren Harris

It all begins with a choice. To embrace each quality of health, ambition, studiousness, involvement, and responsibility, an individual must recognize the power he or she has to choose. While the circumstance may not be ideal, the reaction is a choice. The next factor one must accept is worth. No amount of any quality, positive or negative, will define a person's worth. Furthermore, failure and success can never demean nor increase the worth of a person.

Ambition is the inner drive to work for dreams and goals. Hard work and ambition are needed to reach and even surpass one's goals. As long as I can remember, my childhood dream has always involved performing whether it was dancing, singing, or my own childish version of comedy. Once I found my passion in baton twirling, my dream began to change. While I still loved to perform, I sat in the stands captivated, longing to be on the field twirling with the big girls. After much work, I surpassed my original dream; I had the incredible honor to perform as my school's feature twirler. Although I accomplished my childhood dream, I cannot cease to be ambitious; my dream has to grow and change. I then strove to twirl on the collegiate field and one day to coach twirling. A dream does not simply stop; it progresses. Therefore, ambition can never cease if dreams are to be achieved.

Health begins with a simple statement: as a child of God, I am fearfully and wonderfully made. While I've been made beautiful, taking care of my health can be mentally and physically demanding. Personally, I make efforts to do a session of yoga, drink plenty of water, and complete a measure of fifty sit-ups and squats every day. Yet, the stress of physical health could destroy my mental health if it were a rigid routine; it's all right to miss a day to substitute quality times with significant others. Spiritual health comes into play by one's spending time focusing on relationships and enjoying the time with others. Of course, there are times I am overwhelmed and stressed, but laughter is the best medicine.

Involvement is a mode of hospitality; it shows that one truly cares for others. Plus, it benefits me. Volunteering with preschoolers in church has been one of the most rewarding experiences. I love teaching and getting into mischief with my special helpers and then sitting down for Sunday lunch with a new story to share! Through the marching band and student ambassadors, I am able to help others through similar trials I've experienced, whether helping new students find classes or uplifting school spirit.

The word studious is immediately associated with focus one has on his or her studies, but it is also the willingness to learn and the ability to be taught, not just in subjects or sports, but with people as well. Caring for others is learning about them and their interests and not treating them as a summary on the back of a book. A genuine friendship requires a studious quality.

As noted above, I am many things: a follower of Christ, a student, a mentor, an athlete, and an ambassador. I have incredible responsibility in fulfilling these roles to the best of my capabilities. Not perfect, I take responsibility for my actions and choices to define my character.

Knowing that there is always a little girl watching makes me work even harder as I too was once that little girl.

WAIT A LITTLE LONGER
Jas Clark

As I am looking out this window of life, I heard from the weatherman it's not going to be hot for a few days.

I remember as a kid growing up that our car and truck didn't have air conditioners. I remember one hot summer day; Mama was going to take a sick lady some food and see if she needed anything. I wanted to go.

The car was already hot before we even got in it. I was sitting by the window on the passenger side, and that sun got so hot on my arm it was burning me. I told Mama, "I'm getting in the back seat; the sun is burning my arm."

She told me, "Just stay right where you are — you wanted to ride up here in the front seat, so be patient. The sun will move soon enough, and we are almost there."

By the way, Mama's "almost there" could sometimes take hours. All I thought about was my arm burning and wanting to go to the other side of the car. It wasn't long before the sun was beaming down on the side of the car where I wanted to go, and I had to admit she was right. We delivered the food, and finally the sun was gone. We got back to Granny's and Mama told her, "Please teach this child some patience." I told Granny my arm was burning in the car and all I wanted to do was move to the other side of the car. But

Mama was right, the sun moved just like she said, and in the spot where I had wanted to go.

Granny told me this is what most folks do in life. "They start having a hard time and they are ready to move immediately, blaming it on the place where they are living for causing their misery. And they start over. Everything looks great somewhere else, and today was an example. That sun changed sides with you. Being in another place wouldn't change a thing, unless you have the Lord giving you directions. Sometimes the Lord wants us to stay and wait and see what will happen. You have to be patient and sacrifice for something better that He has in store for you. It might not be overnight but will be worth the wait. If the Lord is making you wait, then be prepared to receive more than you asked for. Everything comes to you in the right moment, when the Lord decides, so be patient and grateful."

Granny walked out to her flower garden and told me to take a good look at all her flowers blooming. "You have asked me a million times when they are going to bloom." She told me that I need to be more like nature — patient. It takes time and patience for these flowers to grow and bloom. "My sweet child, look at this beautiful bloom, the one we have been waiting for. The Lord opened it up on His time, not ours." Granny smiled, wearing her bonnet with her apron tied around her waist and told me, "Now tell your sweet Granny how it was so worth the wait."

It surely was one of the prettiest flowers I've ever seen. I still am working on my patience and remembering what Granny taught me.

And that's why I'm a sinner trying to do better.

SPRING NONSENSE
Dot Day

Clag in May, lime in fall
Out to the tough earth I tread;
The curve of the row, the cut of the hoe
Making new ground to grow and
Surprising me with potatoes and peas
And peppers in pods
And squash in butternut, acorn, patty pan, zucchini,
Also crooked-neck, straight-neck
And a pumpkin or two.

The mosquito kisses my throat and the gnat samples my back —
Merely the torments of harvest near-night.

Sharp and cool and excellent to the eye
Are the rows upon rows: cockleburs, sticker-weed,
Nutgrass, Johnson weed growing wild,
Mingling with morning glories, sawbriers, and tangleweeds,
Embroidered with the bright reds and pinks of Beefsteaks,
Marions, and Betterboys

Dorothy A. Day

  Refusing to lose their places in the sun.
A wavering belief comes forth, rock-solid outer but
     inner-core mouth:
Gardening isn't for vegetables; gardening is for fun!

SPIRITUAL HEART CONDITION

Carl Merchant

Spiritual heart condition — that's a big phrase. What does it mean to have a spiritual heart condition? The Bible talks about a person's heart. First Samuel 16:7 says "But the Lord said to Samuel, 'Do not look on his appearance or the height of his stature, because I have rejected him. For the Lord sees not as man sees; man looks on the outward appearance, but the Lord looks on the heart.'"

Psalm 51:10-2 reads "Create in me a clean heart, O God, and renew a right spirit within me. Cast me not away from your presence and take not your Holy Spirit from me." Here we see the psalmist writing about a spiritual heart condition he was having.

In Ezekiel 36:26-27 the prophet of God tells the people in the land, "I will give you a new heart, and a new spirit I will put within you. And I will remove the heart of stone from your flesh and give you a heart of flesh. And I will put my Spirit within you...." Here we find that Ezekiel was telling the people that if they would follow their spiritual heart condition, they'd see what God was wanting to do for them.

Matthew 7:7-8 reads, "Ask, and it will be given you; seek and you will find; knock, and it will be opened to you. For everyone who asks receives, and the one who seeks finds, and to the one who knocks it will be opened."

Over and over, we see that there is a living God who wants to have a personal relationship with us. But first, we must have a spiritual heart condition when God is placing a call on our hearts to change. Let's look at three people in the Bible who had that spiritual heart condition and wanted to do something about it.

Nicodemus

The first person who had a spiritual heart condition was Nicodemus. His story can be found in John, chapter 3. Nicodemus was a member of the Sanhedrin, the Jewish ruling council. Only the well-educated wealthy and highly respected in the community served on this council. Nicodemus was one of the Pharisees, who were the teachers of the Mosaic law. In short, Nicodemus had spent his entire life teaching the social, religious, and moral standards of his day.

But something started happening to Nicodemus; he started having a spiritual heart condition. He could not at first understand what was going on. He only knew that Jesus, a young rabbi, had come to his town preaching about the Kingdom of God. As Nicodemus listened to Jesus's words, his spiritual heart condition only grew more.

Then, a question grew in Nicodemus. It was exceedingly small, but it was there. More and more the question grew, louder and louder until Nicodemus himself was able to say it. "Have I done everything I can do to go to Heaven?" Before Jesus came to his town, Nicodemus felt confident that he had accomplished enough to get him to Heaven.

But now, Nicodemus had a spiritual heart condition. Many people today walk around with spiritual heart conditions and sadly don't do anything about them. But Nicodemus did want to do something about his condition. That night Nicodemus went to Jesus, not to debate him as the other teachers of the law had done, but to show respect to him. John 3:2-3 reads, "Rabbi, we know you are a teacher who has come from God. For no one could perform the miraculous signs you are doing if God were not with him."

Jesus, knowing all things, turned and looked into Nicodemus' heart and then he said, "I tell you the truth, no one can see the kingdom of God unless he is born again." The words to Nicodemus's question were ringing in his ears as Jesus spoke. John 3:5-8 then says: "Jesus answered, I tell you the truth, no one can enter the kingdom of God unless he is born of water and the Spirit. Flesh gives birth to flesh, but the Spirit gives birth to Spirit."

John 3:13-16 reads, "No one has ever gone into heaven except the one who came from heaven — the Son of Man must be lifted up, that everyone who believes in him may have eternal life. For God so loved the world that he gave his one and only Son, that whoever believes in him shall not perish but have eternal life."

The Sinful Woman

The second person with a heart condition I would like for us to look at can be found in Luke 7:36-50. Here we find a woman whose name is not given; the only title given to her is "sinful woman."

A few years ago, our government ran some television commercial ads about the effects of using illegal drugs. Remember the commercial about the hot frying pan and then someone drops an egg into it and then the egg starts frying? The commentator then says, "This is your brain on drugs; any questions??" But for me, the best TV commercial was filmed in black and white. It was of a camera fixed upon a busy city street. People were walking quickly back and forth to get to their jobs. As the camera slowly moves into the crowd of people, you could hear children talking in the background one by one. "When I grow up, I'm going to be a fireman."

... "When I grow up, I'm going to be a doctor." ... "When I grow up, I'm going to be a lawyer."

Then the camera keeps slowly moving into the crowd until it stops right in front of a street beggar on his knees with his hands raised up asking for money from the people who walked by. Then the camera freezes everybody in the picture, and the commentator speaks: "Nobody says, 'When I grow up, I'm going to be a drug addict.'"

In truth, no one would say that. Nobody says, "When I grow up, I am going to steal from my job and get caught."

Nobody says, "When I grow up, I am going to leave my spouse and kids for somebody else."

Nobody says, "When I grow up, I am going to be addicted to porn or be an alcoholic."

But these things happen. People go down roads where they cannot make a U-turn. Words are said that cannot be taken back; and before you know it, you can be left alone, broken and with a "title" placed on you.

This woman in Luke 7 had the title of a "sinful woman." She had made choices in her past she couldn't go back and change. She had gone down roads she could not return from. But for her, she only knew she had started having a spiritual heart condition.

It all started when Jesus came to her town and started teaching about God's love and the Kingdom of Heaven. Then a question began to grow in the sinful woman. It was exceedingly small, but it was there. More and more the question grew, louder and louder until she was able to say it. "Can I really be forgiven of my sins?" This sinful woman was now ready to do something about her spiritual heart condition.

Simon, a Pharisee, also had been listening to Jesus' sermons and invited Jesus to come eat at his home. Jesus agreed and came into his home and took his place at the table. In Jesus' day the proper invitation for a meal in your home was that the host was to provide water for his guests to wash their feet before reclining at the table. The table was low to the floor, and cushions were used for guests to drop to their knees on. Then the guest would lie on his left hip with his feet behind and use his right hand to eat.

As the sinful woman came into the Pharisee's house to see Jesus, she knelt behind him and started crying on his feet. As she cried, she washed his feet with her tears and then used her hair to dry his feet. Then she started kissing his feet. She then took ointment and anointed his feet with it.

Here is a question to ask yourself. "When was the last time you washed the feet of Jesus with your tears? When was the last time you were truly broken about your sins and asked Jesus to forgive you?"

You might say, "When I got saved, I washed Jesus' feet with my tears," or "When we had a family tragedy, I washed Jesus' feet." But maybe as you read this, you realized you have never really been broken about your sins; you have never asked Jesus to save you.

As Simon the Pharisee was watching all this unfold in his house, he thought to himself, *If Jesus were a prophet, he would know what kind of woman was touching him.*

Jesus knowing all things said, "Simon, I have something to say to you."

Simon answered, "Say it, Teacher."

Jesus said, "A certain moneylender had two debtors. One owed five hundred denarii, and the other fifty. When they could not pay, he cancelled the debt of both. Now which of them will love him more?"

Simon answered, "The one, I suppose, for whom he cancelled the larger debt."

Jesus said to him. "You have judged rightly."

Then turning toward the woman, he said to Simon, "Do you see this woman? I entered your house; you gave me no water for my feet, but she has wet my feet with her tears and wiped them with her hair. You gave me no kiss, but from the time I came in she has not ceased to kiss my feet. You did not anoint my head with oil, but she has anointed my feet with ointment. Therefore, I tell you, her sins, which are many, are forgiven — for she loved much."

Then he said to her, "Your sins are forgiven."

That night, as the woman left Simon's house, she still had a "label." Life for her would still be a struggle, but now, God was living in her heart. Maybe for the first time there was true peace and joy in her life.

The Rich, Young Ruler

The story of the next person with a spiritual heart condition can be found in the books of Matthew, Mark, and Luke. Here we find this man is not named like the sinful woman, but he is described with three terms we all wish we had. The Bible says he was rich. Oh, to be rich; never to have to worry about if you have enough money to pay your bills. Then the writer says he was young. Wow! To be rich and young at the same time. You would be able to see and do all the things in life you want. But we are not done; the Bible also says he was a ruler. You would think to be rich and young would be enough, but to have people listen and do what you say is like icing on a cake.

And now, we find this man started having a spiritual heart condition. The only thing that has changed in his life is that Jesus has come to his town, teaching and preaching about God's love and the Kingdom of God. As the rich young ruler listened to Jesus's words, his spiritual heart condition only grew more and more. Then, just like the other examples we have looked at, a question grew in his heart. It was exceedingly small, but it was there. More and more the question grew, louder and louder until he himself was able to say it. "When I die, will I go to Heaven?"

Remember, as said before, many of us are walking around today with a spiritual heart condition. For some of us, we will do what it takes to come to the foot of the cross and ask Jesus to forgive us of our sins and live a life pleasing to him. But some are still waiting.

In the book of Mark 10:17-20, we find the young ruler running to Jesus and falling at his feet. He asked Jesus what he must do to inherit eternal life. Jesus told the young man, "You know the commandments: 'Do not murder, do not commit adultery, do not steal, do not give false testimony, do not defraud, honor your father and mother.' The young man replied: 'Teacher, all these I have kept since I was a boy.'"

Then Jesus does something he does with all of us. He looks into the young man's heart. There Jesus found doors that were completely open, but one door in his heart was closed. Then as Lord of Lords and King of Kings, Jesus walks through the door to see what is on the other side. Then Jesus told the young ruler, "Sell all that you have and give to the poor. And then come and follow me."

For many years I have read this scripture and only thought about how rich people will have a hard time going to heaven. But I believe there is a lot more to God's word here.

You see, Jesus, no matter how much He loves us, will not take second place in our lives. An example of this is found in Luke 9:57-62 — "As they were walking along the road, a man said to him, 'I will follow you wherever you go.'

"Jesus replied, 'Foxes have holes and birds of the air have nests, but the Son of Man has no place to lay his head.'"

"Jesus said to another man, 'Follow me.'"

"But the man replied, 'Lord, first let me go and bury my father.'"

"Jesus said to him. 'Let the dead bury their own dead, but you go and proclaim the kingdom of God.'"

"Still another said, "I will follow you, Lord; but first let me go back and say good-bye to my family.'"

"Jesus replied, 'No one who puts his hand to the plow and looks back is fit for service in the Kingdom of God.'"

You see, for some of us, we call ourselves Christians; we do all the right things like the young ruler did, but maybe we keep a door of our heart closed. We don't want to open that door for anyone but ourselves; and somehow, we think Jesus will understand. We still want to hang on to a bad habit, a bank account, an unhealthy relationship ... The list can go on and on.

Do you ever wonder how the rich young ruler felt to be told this? Mark 10:22 says of the man — "His face fell, and he went away sad because he had great wealth."

Has there ever been a time God's Holy Spirit convicted you about sin hidden behind a door of your heart, and you refused to give it to Jesus? Then you already know how this young ruler felt.

As we look at these three Bible characters, we find that they all came to Jesus looking for answers. The scriptures show that the sinful woman came to Jesus wanting forgiveness at any cost. The rich young ruler wanted to be saved, but when the cost of his salvation meant giving up something he coveted, he went away sad.

But what about Nicodemus? John 3 doesn't tell us what decision he made. We do see in John 7:45 that the chief priests and Pharisees wanted Jesus arrested and his ministry stopped. Nicodemus was one of those members there, and he stood up for Jesus in their meeting.

In John 19:38-42, we see Jesus has gone to the cross and died for our sins. The plan that God the Father had made for Jesus was carried out and accomplished.

"After these things Joseph of Arimathea, who was a disciple of Jesus, but secretly for fear of the Jews, asked Pilate that he might take away the body of Jesus, and Pilate gave him permission. So, he came and took away his body. Nicodemus also, who earlier had come to Jesus by night, came bringing a mixture of myrrh and aloes, about seventy-five pounds in weight. So, they took the body of Jesus and bound it in linen cloths with the spices, as is the burial custom of the Jews. Now in the place where he was crucified there was a garden, and in the garden a new tomb in which no one had yet been laid. So, because of the Jewish day of Preparation, since the tomb was close at hand, they laid Jesus there."

I often wonder why the Bible says Nicodemus brought seventy-five pounds of myrrh and aloes. Why was it important that it be recorded in the Bible? Doing some online research, I discovered that the value of the seventy-five pounds of myrrh and aloes in today's pricing would have been anywhere from $150,000 to $200,000. That was a great expense for Nicodemus to have made for a young radical rabbi. Yet we still see him dedicating his time and money and working with Joseph to prepare the body.

A proper Jewish burial meant that the body be thoroughly washed and cleaned. That would mean both men would have to wash Jesus' hair, carefully removing any broken thorns that might have come from the crown of thorns the Roman soldiers placed on him. Then both men would have to wash the body, cleaning the sand, rocks, and dried blood out of each cut and gash Jesus had. Then the spices that Nicodemus brought were applied on the body and wrapped in linen.

That evening, both men who were high-ranking Jewish religious leaders had completed their task and walked out of Jesus' tomb. They knew that touching a dead body would disqualify them from the upcoming Jewish Passover. They were not going to be able to sit in their respected places on that day and be seen and heard. Did Nicodemus become a disciple of Jesus? Did Nicodemus finally understand the words of Jesus that night in John chapter 3? Did Nicodemus become born again?

Well ... only his heart knows for sure.

SEVEN YEARS OUT
Janet Taylor-Perry

Bret Perry is seven years out.

The phrase "seven years out" means nothing to people who have never suffered from cancer or had a loved one battle the disease. However, to a cancer survivor the term means the same as life. Many famous names come to mind as cancer survivors, such as Christina Applegate, Lance Armstrong, Howie Mandel, Martina Navratilova, and Mandy Patinkin. Although famous people bring attention to the subject, close friends or family make it real.

To watch a loved one survive recurring cancer has a major impact on a person.

Bret was first diagnosed with colon cancer seven years ago. He underwent surgery and rounds of chemotherapy. He received a good prognosis and thought he had dodged the bullet. At a later checkup, the cancer had returned but not in his colon. This time the cells were in his liver.

After numerous treatments of radiation and chemotherapy, once again the devastating disease seemed to have been defeated. Bret was weak and understandably changed from having undergone the ordeal. He lost every hair on his head and a great deal of weight. Nonetheless, his outlook on life remained positive. He never gave up. His smile stayed real; his eyes still twinkled with boyish mischief. Bret's attitude impressed many people.

Bret appeared to have won another battle. A few visits to the doctor looked good.

Then, the shocker came. Although Bret had never smoked a cigarette in his life, cancer attacked his lungs. Bret had another fight to endure. Through it all, he inspired many.

Health professionals who have treated him did not give him until the end of 2011. Bret is still alive. He has held his three granddaughters, and the last time I saw Bret, it was at an unexpected family funeral for which he flew in to be a pall bearer. Although no longer an actual family member, Bret's embrace of me lingered. No words needed to be spoken for both of us to say, "I will always love you."

At the last report, Bret's cancer had not left, but it had not grown. Nobody has a clue what caused these various forms of cancer. Could it be the cadmium he was exposed to for so many years in working with carbide tools? Could it be something he came in contact with during his research for Pfizer? There is no answer.

Bret Perry's face will never appear on the cover of *Time, Newsweek,* or *Sports Illustrated* as a cancer survivor or as an inspiration to millions because he is not famous. He is merely a friend, a son, a husband, a father, a grandfather, a brother, a nephew, a grandson, a son-in-law, and an uncle. If this beast called cancer finally defeats him, he will not be on the national news. Bret will be an unsung hero. Yet, he has influenced many in at least two states, his home state of Mississippi, and Connecticut, his chosen state of residence. His optimism and fortitude, his humor and determination, his love and devotion have warmed hearts and surprised caregivers. Bret Perry is seven years out.

End Note

Bret lost his eight-year battle with cancer. He was able to travel once again to Mississippi to give his elder daughter in marriage on March 23, 2013. He looked so good at a casual glance nobody would have known he had less than two months to live after stage IV colon cancer metastasized to his spine. He turned forty-eight on April 23 and celebrated the birth of a grandson with his younger daughter on April 24. Just after midnight on May 19, he passed peacefully into Eternity, surrounded by most of his family. On May 22, loved ones celebrated a life worth living, and Bret's ashes were scattered at the softball fields of East Lyme, Connecticut, a place where he touched many lives.

I was not among those who bade Bret farewell, but for me, he will always live in my heart and memory. And he was much more than an inspiration to me.

CINQUAIN: SENSORY POEMS

Hazel R. James Lonie

Memories are cloudy, pale and blue
Melted marshmallows leave a sweet taste
Muffled sounds of forks, knives and spoons
Merge glorious aromas and dazzling flavors
Mingled with deception, nonappreciation and lies
Monologues cloak the dirty dust of the past.

Harriet sees with an omnipotence now
Hatred grows a bitter aftertaste
Haunting voices speak a horrible truth
Hell stews rotted deeds; a stench untold
Hope is a beacon larger than life
How will things ever change?

Writing wasn't my first choice for an occupation; for a hobby either. My confidence fluctuated many times during group presentations. By this time though, stepping outside my comfort zone had become a new means of challenging the limits of life. I distributed my work to the group, finished reading the piece above and waited for critique.

Dorothy A. Day

"I thought cinquains had five lines; this has six," the tenor voice sounded its critique.

That wasn't the response I'd anticipated. It was embarrassing. The poem came from an old pamphlet given to me many years ago. On several occasions when money and time were short, personalized gifts had magically emerged from this booklet. Were those gifts cinquains? Assumption proved to be dangerous, the tenor voice spoke the truth. The unnamed-incomplete poem had six lines in each verse.

Days passed after that incident, and it continued to haunt me. Late one evening, I arrived at a church gathering early to get a suitable parking place. Dim light soon faded to a scattered darkness, illuminated by the shadow-making lights of the parking lot. I stared at the old writing document given to me about fourteen years ago. My obsession with the people at the workshop, the pamphlet itself and my perceptions of what took place that day held me spellbound. The mysterious lighting of dusk helped to heighten my senses during the meditative experience. I defied nightfall and continued to read. Light, time and a space to think proved to be proper nourishment for my spirited soul.

Memory faltered but evidence gave concrete answers as I scanned the pages: Grace House, a non-profit HIV/AIDS Transitional Facility, Writers Workshop, Mississippi State Hospital Community Services, Stubbs Homeless Program, © 2006.

I know even if I'd heard or read this part of the information, it didn't touch me in the slightest. I was a different person in those days. I believed and still believe, open to the public means everybody — I'm Harriet Q. Public, therefore I was an acceptable person as part of any public gathering.

At this point, I relinquished control to Harriet and gave her the mental space to relive that Saturday morning in November of 2006. She remembered the air felt cooler than expected, so she took her black dress blazer off and put on a faded navy blue sweat jacket as she arrived at the Eudora Welty Library on State Street. The hood was probably better any way; it would help to keep the cold air out of her ears and face. Laser surgery a week or so earlier made it sensible to use part of the hood to cover her healing eye.

The writing workshop took place in the conference room on the other side of the children's reading area. The area wasn't new to Harriet; it was the location where she'd attended other workshops and exhibited some of her artwork during her art association days. She entered the room and ...

White people.

Several ladies and one man sat at a long rectangular table when Harriet entered. She took a seat to the right of the lady on the left end. She assumed the man on the other end of the table would lead the workshop.

I ain't sitting next to the leader ... A white man, no way.

Wrong assumption — the lady to her left was the leader. Susie Miss Leader will do to give her a name. Susie announced, "It's time to start" and introduced herself. The others followed clockwise around the table giving their names, where they were from, and a tidbit of personal information.

"I'm Harriet Love, I'm from Jackson," is all I said.

Susie went on to the "Waking Up" lesson on page three. She read, then instructed us to write about the same topic. Harriet followed her instructions; wrote about the cold bathroom, getting dressed, and a quick breakfast that morning. In clockwise order, Harriet was last when it was time to read.

These Southerners seemed to know each other. They were friendly enough, but Harriet couldn't shake a strange feeling about them.

Crayons and watercolor brushes were placed on the table with small containers of water. The leader went into great detail explaining about a crayon-resist.

Dorothy A. Day

Harriet remembered thinking the activity wasn't a serious assignment for adults.

What's she so excited about? Kindergarten children do this.

Harriet remained polite; maybe the others needed Susie's instructions.

The others began to chatter, amazed by the fact that Harriet was able to draw with a crayon without using a pencil first.

Am I a specimen of some sort, being examined, being measured by some unknown criteria? I could get this treatment in other places. I'm being categorized for some reason.

Harriet completed applying the heavy layers of crayon and proceeded to use the brushes without further instruction.

These aren't the right brushes for this activity.

"You've done this before," one of the ladies said.

"Yes." Harriet wasn't in a mood to give further comment. After twenty-eight years of insults and disrespect while teaching art, she'd wandered about since her retirement last June trying to find traction. She sought to find a "new self" without the rigors of employment and now to be in this predicament.

The group did some sort of a pre-writing discussion exercise after the creative activity. Miss Leader gave the word, "brain," and each person gave a synonym for it. With the simpler responses taken, my answer was, "Cerebral."

General Foghorn, lit up all ecstatic and he blurted out, "You said cerebral."

You go to hell.

Harriet glared at him. "Yes, I did."

Susie Miss Leader seemed to sense the friction and changed the subject. The other hens were speechless. After a pause, they found their voices and talked to each other while Harriet peeked at each of them trying to assess their attitude and purpose.

"We're going to break for lunch now. We'll finish with poetry at one," Susie said.

Abruptly, Harriet left the table and headed to the Baptist HealthPlex further north on State Street. She'd learned to live in her car as a traveling teacher, so everything needed was readily available. Lunch was a granola bar with something to drink as she drove. She'd worn her old tennis shoes. With her jacket already changed, the transition for the quick walk was an easy one.

The afternoon session concluded without a feeling of attachment to any of the other participants. Harriet and I've thought about them on and off through the years when I've used the writing booklet. We've always blamed them for our ill-feelings. Somehow as I sat in the darkness of the car that evening, a new light dawned on the events of that day and other days since. It was true, I mislabeled the sensory poem as a cinquain.

Perceptions are a two-way street. Assumptions, preconceived notions, and prejudice are some of the suitable descriptors for what took place during the Grace House Writers' Workshop in 2006. Thinking about it now in 2020, neither side really tried to know the other. The workshop, even though advertised as open to the public, was intended for poor homeless people in the area. How could the presenter politely ask me, "Are you homeless? Do you have HIV/AIDS?"

I'd unintentionally presented Harriet to them with the right lens missing from her glasses, (The Nigerian medical assistant had taken the lens out of my glasses after surgery saying I didn't need the medicated lens any longer.), a wrinkled-faded navy blue sweat jacket, and a pair of old stained tennis shoes. My clothes were functional. They were clean. They were exercise clothing, however, not casual or business dress.

Harriet was viewed by people who didn't know her. How could they understand the logic of her actions? Harriet could've introduced herself as a retired art teacher who lived in the old Van Winkle area of Jackson, but that didn't happen.

Harriet had grown accustomed to being defensive in many areas of her life, and she protected herself. She'd unfairly judged these people as "White people" who came to polish their egos by mingling with poor Black people from the loftiness of their superiority.

Ol' Harriet came to them with a twenty-eight-year-old chip on her shoulder about art. American education even today fails to give proper respect to the tremendous value of art and creativity in its curriculums. Susie Miss Leader didn't mean any harm with her crayon-resist project. It was an economical, quick exercise. Susie didn't intend to construct a dissertation on the greater ramifications of life with the activity.

Clearly, given the time and space to relive objectively the writing workshop, I, Harriet Green-Love realized I wasn't the innocent participant I thought I was. Perhaps if Ol' Harriet had properly introduced herself and behaved differently, then she'd be able to remember the names or faces of some of the others in the workshop. And, her first writing experience would be remembered with pleasure. Harriet and I are of one spirit these days.

Unfortunately, we weren't in 2006. Life has revealed itself in layers as Harriet has evolved through the years of her journey. The Great Spirit gave this time, in a new light and space to reveal to Ol' Harriet that her behavior contributed to her problems. Years of turmoil are laid to rest in one body, mind, and spirit.

MOTIVATIONAL ANALYSIS: DOROTHY DAY

Madalyn Sheridan Clark

Introduction

Having the privilege to have met someone that has faced insurmountable odds and still come out on top is inspiring. Being able to take a negative situation and turn it around into something positive is one of the most admirable attributes a person can have. Dorothy Ainsworth Day has been doing this, every day, for over 15 years; most of the people that know her would say she has been doing it her whole life. She has been diagnosed with Inclusion Body Myositis and has had to completely change how she lives her day-to-day life. What is behind her motivation to continue to overcome these odds?

Simply, the answer is the need to belong and the need for autonomy. These two intrinsic motivators are what have made her successful in overcoming these insurmountable odds. The need to belong and the need for autonomy are what keep her going every day and inspires her to keep trying new things, regardless of her disability.

Dorothy A. Day

Background

Dorothy Ainsworth Day is from a small town in Mississippi called Crystal Springs. She was born March 16, 1949. She is married to Charles Day, with whom she had two daughters: those two daughters gave Day four grandchildren. Growing up, she dreamed of teaching English to high school students. To fulfill that dream, she attended Mississippi College and received two degrees. Her first degree is in Secondary English education and her second one is in marriage and family counseling. For over 25 years she taught English to hundreds of students. In 2005 tragedy struck. At the age of 56, Dot Day was diagnosed with a form of Myositis. After many years and many tests, it was determined that she had Inclusion Body Myositis which causes muscle weakness, usually in the muscles closest to the trunk of the body (MedlinePlus). Day and her family were devastated.

At first, the effects of the disease were not very harsh on Day but everyone knew that, more than likely, they were going to get worse. Slowly, but surely, the disease started taking over her muscles. It started with her walking with a cane, but then having a bad fall on the way into church. This led to walking with a walker that she was able to walk a full 5k for an event benefiting Myositis awareness; this was very exciting for Day and her family. A few years later, however, she was put in a motorized chair and that is how she has had to get around since. Day went from being a very active member in her community, including singing in the church choir, participating in the town's Tomato Festival, and teaching at the high school, to being unable to get out of the house but once a week because of fatigue.

Through all of this adversity, Dot Day has still prevailed. Because she was able to get her second degree in marriage and family counseling, she is now able to spend her time helping others. Whether she realizes it or not, while she is helping others, she is helping herself by still providing herself with social interaction. If you ask her, her greatest achievement, other than her family, would be writing and publishing her book about family history, *Memories of the Sharecropper's Family* (Day 2017). She had always wanted to be a writer and when she was no longer able to teach English, she took her English degree and used it to write her book. These examples, and many more, are evidence for Day's success.

The Need to Belong

After speaking with Day, she explained that after her diagnosis and living with the incurable disease's effects for over 15 years, her main goal was to redefine her purpose in life (Day 2020). Her children were gone with their own families, she could not teach anymore, and she could not fully participate in anything around the city. Her motivation to find her new purpose points to the human need to belong. As humans, we have a fundamental need to belong. According to Edward and Melissa Burkley, the need to belong is defined as "a pervasive drive to form and maintain lasting, positive interpersonal relationships" and according to Baumeister and Leary, the need to belong is "an innate drive that causes emotional, physiological, and behavioral changes." (Burkley & Burkley, 2018, 7.1; Baumeister & Leary, 1995).

In order to fulfill this need to belong, she started by making behavioral changes. Day tried her hand at art. Her husband set up a space in his shop for her to paint. She enjoyed this because it helped her pass the time; however, it did not end up fulfilling her need to belong because there was no interaction with others and she soon had to quit, again because of the lack of muscle control in her arms. She then picked up the hobby of making quilts for "Quilts of Honor," a non-profit organization that supplies veterans with quilts. She much enjoyed this because it was time consuming and she was able to do it with others. Again, she was not able to stick with it because the lack of muscle control limited her ability to cut fabric. Even though she was not able to find her new purpose with these things, she still maintained motivation and found other paths to fulfill her need to belong.

As previously stated, she capitalized on her degree in marriage and family counseling. She is able to meet weekly with different clients and help them through any struggles with their marriage or within their family. This is her newfound purpose. Through this platform, she is able to do something for others while engaging in social interaction. Social interaction is something she misses much and being able to do so on a weekly basis gets her closer to fulfilling her need to belong. Also previously stated, something she had always wanted was to write a book and it be published. That wish came true with her book, *Memories of the Sharecropper's Family*. When she is not meeting with clients, she is writing her books. She is currently working on a biography about veterans. What comes with that is meeting with different veterans and speaking with them about their experiences; this also provides Day with meaningful interactions with others.

The Need for Autonomy

Another form of motivation for Day was the need for autonomy. According to Burkley, the need for autonomy is "a desire for freedom, personal control, and free choice." (Burkley & Burkley 5.1). Considering autonomy is one of the core human motives, it is very important that Day fulfill this need. One of the criteria for a core human motive is that it should result in positive outcomes that enable survival. In Day's case, she was experiencing a lack of fulfillment for this core human motive which resulted in negative outcomes, which tend to threaten survival (Burkley & Burkley).

When Day found out her diagnosis, one of her major fears was the loss of independence. She states that a very hard step for her was giving up driving. Because of her disease, she became unable to move safely and easily into the driver's seat, and then eventually unable to lift her foot enough to control the accelerator and brake. This was just the start of Day seeing a decrease in her fulfillment of her need for autonomy.

The Day family are known to be headstrong and independent. They are not good at asking others for help and prefer to do things on their own. Day went from having her need for autonomy completely fulfilled, to slowly becoming more and more unfulfilled. One can see why this was a large feat for Day to overcome. She has very limited control over her own body. Since being put in her chair, she can no longer get in or out of bed, use the bathroom, or prepare dinner on her own. She struggles daily with finding a way to gain her independence and control of her own life. To attempt once again to have her fulfill her need for autonomy, she decided that she needed to find a way to start making her own choices again and gain independence in new activities.

Autonomy motivates one to think creatively because of being in control and not being affected by the influence of others. Day uses this motivation to think creatively in her day-to-day life. Through all of the adversity she has faced, she has never lost her sense of creativity. From writing her books to sewing and quilting to painting, she has not let her disease hold her back. When one door closes for her, she always manages to find another door to open. Choosing to spend her time with these previously stated activities, Day is able to find her sense of control again. Even though there is a lot Day cannot control, she has managed to find control in the little things. She also makes sure that she at least tries to do tasks like getting out of bed on her own and making dinner without help, because that helps build her sense of independence.

Intrinsic Motivation

With all that being said, Day's major motives came intrinsically. Intrinsic motivation is completing an action for internal reasons. One feels internal satisfaction for completing an activity without the need for external inducement for completion (Morey, 2017, p.19). Day knew that she needed to find something that brings her joy, since she could no longer participate in everything that had brought her that feeling before her diagnosis. The need to belong and the need for autonomy both fall under intrinsic motivation. They are needs that come from within that motivate one to succeed. These are needs that we somewhat unconsciously fulfill. In Day's case, this means she knew she needed to find her new purpose and a new sense of independence, but not why she felt the need to do those things.

Conclusion

In conclusion, Dorothy Ainsworth Day has been faced with insurmountable odds and has been able to motivate herself to overcome these odds. After being diagnosed with Inclusion Body Myositis and living with its difficulties for over 15 years, Day has since changed the way she lives her life in every way. What she has used to motivate herself against these odds are two intrinsic motivators known as the need to belong and the need for autonomy. To fulfill the need to belong, she found her new purpose in counseling those with family struggles and writing two books. To fulfill her need for autonomy, she has taken advantage of the little things that she is able to do on her own and spends most of her time focused on those. She also at least tries to do the big things on her own on her good days so that she can feel more independent. Day is a prime example of how one is able to take a negative situation and bring something positive out of it.

References

Baumeister, R. F. & Leary, M. R. (1995) *The need to belong: Desire for interpersonal attachments as a fundamental human motivation.* (pp. 117, 497-529). Psychological Bulletin.

Burkley, E. (2018). 5.1 Autonomy. In 1051849516 803204463 M. Burkley (Ed.), *Motivation Science*. New York, NY: Pearson.

Burkley, E. (2018). 7.1 Belonging. In 1051849516 803204463 M. Burkley (Ed.), *Motivation Science*. New York, NY: Pearson.

Day, D. (2020, November 13). Dot Day and Dealing with Inclusion Body Myositis [Telephone interview].

Gagne, M. (2000). *The role of autonomy support and autonomy orientation in the internalization of autonomous regulation for prosocial behavior* (Master's thesis, University of Rochester, 2000) (p. iv). Ann Arbor, MI: ProQuest.

Morey, R. (2017). *A Path to Motivation: A Mediated Moderation Analysis of the Relationships between Task-Contingent Rewards, Psychological Ownership, and Intrinsic Motivation Using Path Analysis* (Doctoral dissertation, Long Island University, 2017) (pp. 1-157). Ann Arbor, MI: ProQuest.

Myositis | Polymyositis | Dermatomyositis. (2020, July 08). Retrieved November 13, 2020, from https://medlineplus.gov/myositis.html

WHAT'S YOUR FAVORITE CUP OF TEA?

Jas Clark

As I am looking out this window of life, I remember every Sunday morning my mama getting her five tea bags out and putting them in a pan to boil to make plenty of sweet, sweet tea for after church. She put in lots of sugar to make her sweet tea. If you ever had it, you would have loved it.

My Granny didn't drink it all the time, but every now and then she asked me to bring her a little of Mama's tea. After church one Sunday, I took Granny some tea. She heated it up and told me that she knew that I wasn't a hot tea person. She smiled and told me, "That's all right; it's just not your cup of tea. Life is sorta like a cup of tea, but there is a little difference though." She laughed and laughed and told me all folks will love you when they get in hot water, just like teabags. She told me that we can make tea ourselves, and if we don't like it, we can just throw it out.

Sometimes in life without the Lord, we can't do that. With life's "cup of tea," we have to drink it. When we have to drink those bitter cups of life, we all do have a choice of how to drink that bitterness on down. Granny told me there is a way to help with life's bitterness. "You get to know the Lord, and He will strain that tea for you and make the bitterness go away."

When I look back over all my years of my life, I've drunk a lot of life's bitter tea. I had a lot this past weekend. Granny told me when your tea is bitter, ask the Lord to put His sweetness in it. Granny told me all of us have different teas to drink. Granny got out an old tea strainer and told me the new tea bags now are filters for the tea, but a long while back, you had old metal filters to strain your coffee and your tea.

You always need the "Father-From-Up-Above-Filter" for your entire life, or life will stay bitter. He will filter out discouragement, fear, anxiety, depression, sadness, anger, resentment — and He will sweeten your bitter tea with His pure love, sweeter than honey. Granny told me He doesn't care if you are drinking out of fine china cups, or one with cracks, chips, faded color, crackled finish, or a broken handle. It will still hold your tea, and He will sweeten it.

We will not be everyone's cup of tea, but we are all the Lord's — made in His image, and we all want our cups filled with the Lord. We want it filled with love, peace, joy, and happiness. We all have a tea maker with a built-in strainer — and it's the Lord. I'm getting Him to filter my bitter tea, and that's why I'm a sinner trying to do better.

Fill up someone's teacup today with the Lord.

MY GRANDMOTHER'S LOVE
Caryl Hackler

She plants the seeds
without us knowing.
Then she will see for herself
if we are growing.
The stitches of my life
are sewn together with love.
And as I grow and learn
I thank the Lord above
That I have received
my grandmother's love.

MISSION ACCEPTED

Larry McAlpin

*And they overcame him by the blood of the Lamb and
by the word of their testimony,
and they did not love their lives to the death.
Revelation 12:11*

I have been in church as long as I can remember, so I heard about God all my life. I accepted Jesus Christ as my savior at age 16. Soon after that, I did some very stupid stuff in my teenage years. Afterward, I was walking and praying to God asking Him to get me out of the bad situation I was in.

I told God, "I will do anything for You, or go anywhere for You if you deliver me from my foolish actions." Then I said, "But I will never go to Africa."

Fast forward 50 years. I am retired, and I am a very active believer in Jesus Christ. He is my Savior and Lord. My pastor goes to Zimbabwe, Africa, on mission trips about twice every year. One Sunday, I was convicted and convinced that I should go with him to Zimbabwe on his next mission trip. He set a solid date and let me know. I told him that I would think about it and let him know if I planned to go. I remember my dealing with God at age 16 and was having second thoughts about my going on this mission trip.

While trying to make up my mind, my daily activities kept going. I even received a word from a couple people and in my spirit: "I am the hands and feet of Jesus."

I have some land and farm equipment to work it. Some brush on the north side of the land needed to be cleared out. I got on my tractor/backhoe one morning heading to the north side. My heart was filled with joy and happiness as I started out of the barn.

I love God's nature and all its beauty, so I was very fulfilled that morning. As I drove across my acre pond dam, I glanced in the water's edge to see a beautiful big fish jumping. I was saying, "Thank you, Father, for all your natural beauty."

When I looked up back on the trail ahead, I saw my front tractor tire go over the edge of the dam into the water. Then the tractor/backhoe fell over into the pond with me on it. As I hit the water, I was able to get out of the way of the metal tractor top before it pinned me to the pond bottom.

As I swam to the shore, I heard, in my spirit, "The devil is trying to take you out because great things will happen in Zimbabwe because of your hands and feet being owned by Jesus." I got onshore and said, "Yes, Lord. I am going to Zimbabwe."

Later after telling my pastor that I definitely was going, he called me with flight information for my airline ticket to Zimbabwe. I asked what it would cost me. He replied, "Nothing. Someone has taken care of the cost of your airline ticket to and from Zimbabwe."

I have no idea how and who paid my airfare, but it was another confirmation.

I went on the mission trip to Africa and witnessed many wonderful things. People were saved and delivered from witchcraft. Also, a new church was established in a small village in the bush in southeast Zimbabwe. I saw an outdoor baptism with people lining up to get in the water at the river. On either side of the center of the river where the baptisms were taking place, I noticed people standing and throwing rocks.

Their actions seemed distracting and out of place. I questioned someone nearby. "They throw the rocks to keep the crocodiles away."

People were hungry for the Gospel. It was amazing.

BIG HEART

Dot A. Day

Marshall had made his way through a variety of jobs and a failed marriage and was now a fledgling entrepreneur with his own carpet-cleaning service. Peering intently through the rain-smeared windshield, the blond thirtyish workman drove his new maroon van toward Pearl and his home.

A front had pushed the wind from the west to the north, and the result was biting cold and what was becoming a forceful rain. As he headed south on I-55, a fender bender gave him time to look around.

As he inched along, keeping a wary eye on the car ahead, he noticed them — a trio headed north on foot beside the frontage road, a woman with two children. The woman was bent forward. The wet group slogged along the verge, pushing into the wind. Each child was carrying a garbage bag over his shoulder. The young woman carried two items, a full black garbage sack over her shoulder and a hard-body suitcase.

The temperature'll drop even more as night comes on. It's gonna be cold.

His mind flashed to those times of intense, wet misery on the farm. One time in particular ....

Sonny was twelve, attempting to do a man's work on the farm and attend school. His father's recent heart attack had resulted in his being weak and easily fatigued. The old farmhouse had a deep well without an electric pump, but they did have electricity, and two large firewood boxes demanding daily filling. The milk cows and hogs requested feeding with incessant mooing and snorting. Dot, his ten-year-old sister, helped with some of the work and tended the chickens.

Still, the two children recognized that their work was important, and they absorbed the lesson that struggle was necessary for survival. The two were the youngest of eight children, six of whom had already left home for their military service, college, marriage, or careers.

The first to leave home had been Marvin. One day after his high school graduation, he joined his siblings in the cotton patch to chop cotton. He worked for a short time. Without any detailing of his plans, he threw down his hoe. He changed his clothes, hitched a ride into Collins where he decided to get to the Air Force recruiters. After his years of obligation to Uncle Sam were complete, he used the GI bill to attend Mississippi Southern College.

Marvin moved from graduating with a history education degree to a job as teacher and basketball coach at Williamsburg High School. He left teaching after a couple of years to open a store with a friend. From there he moved into banking. Daddy was as proud of Marvin's success as Marvin was, proudly talking about his banker son. Daddy was not lavish with praise or affection, and Marvin did not hear the pride reflected by his comments because the comments were not to him nor made in his presence.

Others praised his business acumen. The president of the bank told him, "Marvin, stick with us. You'll go far in banking. You haven't made a bad loan yet." The words cemented his loyalty and his desire to continue as he had started. His efforts paid off in his becoming a young vice-president of the regional bank. The promotion was celebrated with a new Buick, not a second-hand Ford.

Although his parents and younger siblings had a telephone, he elected to visit rather than call and tell of his promotion. Funny — he at 32 was still looking for his dad's approval. He, his wife, and two young sons would make the trip from Rankin to Simpson County that afternoon. He looked down at his carefully creased trousers, his white shirt with the cuffs rolled up almost to his elbows, his polished wingtips. *Daddy'll be proud of me now.*

Marvin nosed the Buick onto the long gravel driveway running alongside New Hope Road, hoping not to get it too dusty before showing it off. He parked in the shade of the large oak tree, not far from the woodpile where Dot was stacking firewood onto Sonny's outstretched arms.

"I wonder who's in that big car." The front doors of the shiny sedan opened in answer to Dot's mumble. She ran to the house to announce the arrival. As Marvin and Ann opened the back doors to get out the boys, ages two and four, Sonny deposited the firewood in the wood box on the front porch. All met at the car to admire it and to hear of Marvin's achievement.

Sonny peered into the driver's side to better see the instrument panel. "Sonny Boy, don't you get into my car with those nasty shoes on. I don't want my car messed up."

Sonny's face reddened. He looked down at his shoes and after-school work clothes. They couldn't afford work shoes and school shoes, so he was using old sneakers wired together to keep the front sole on one. They looked nasty, but he cleaned them after his work with the livestock was finished. Left out on the back porch to dry, they were clean enough to put back on the next day to step again into the mud and manure. They afforded little protection for his feet but were better than nothing. *If he has money enough for a big car, he could buy me some boots ... my brother Joe would.*

Dorothy A. Day

"Come on, Dot, let's finish our work." Dot followed him to the wood pile to load more split oak onto the arms of her brother.

"Why does he think he is so much better than we are?" Marshall's embarrassment hardened into anger.

"I don't care if he gets to be president of the company, he's not supposed to treat people like that. He has no right to treat us like animals. I wouldn't be that ugly to a dog," he vented.

The two separated, Dot to the henhouse and Sonny to the pigsty where the squealing and grunting attempted to dissuade him of his shame.

His thoughts continued to center on his humiliation. *If he has money enough for a big car, he could buy me some boots.*

They completed the tasks, expecting to have Marvin's family join them for supper. They didn't, stopping only to show the car and visit a short time with the parents.

Twenty years later, Sonny had grown into his name Marshall. He still remembered those days of cold, wet misery. He couldn't just leave them there. More minutes passed as he remembered the days of physical misery and the toll of poverty and feeling the pinch of not feeling as good as others.

Marshall did not see any cars stalled on the side of the road, so he took the first exit and pointed the van northward.

"Hey, y'all get in out of the rain," he shouted as he opened the sliding door of the passenger side. The woman looked up from the mudhole she was navigating the young girl through to the van where the voice of the man offered help. "I've needed help before; come on; get in."

The young woman helped the young girl settle into the second seat, then slid onto the front seat while the freckled-face boy climbed in, a rooster tail of mud and dampness following.

"I really appreciate you stoppin'. I'm trying to get to Memphis. We started out in a car, but it broke down in Wiggins, so we just left it. We've been hitching all day."

They drove a couple of miles farther. She broke the silence.

"My name's Susan, and these two are Beth Ann and John Mark. Sorry 'bout the mess we're makin."

Marshall's face flushed as he introduced himself. He apologized for the clutter of hoses and other cleaning materials. "This is my carpet-cleaning van; no need to worry about any mess."

He was getting back onto the interstate and noticed the tears flowing down her already-wet face past a bruise fading to a greenish blotch near her temple.

"I bet you're hungry," he said to the kids. "Open that cooler back there and see if there's anything there you want." While the two, a pre-teen boy and a pre-school girl occupied themselves with the fruit in there, he resumed his talk and tried to figure a plan beyond getting them out of the rain.

He adjusted the heater and tried to figure a plan beyond getting them out of the rain.

"Did you have any plans about where to stay for the night?"

"I planned to be at my mother's in Memphis, so I didn't have plans or money to make plans. I've been thinking all afternoon about sleeping under a bridge once we got through Jackson or seeing if someone at a truck stop would let us stay in the restaurant."

"I can't take you home with me. I live in the wrong direction. In Pearl." Marshall didn't tell her he and his wife had divorced and he had custody of two young children.

"Is there anyone able to get your car or help you?"

"No, there's no one available to help. I'm pretty sure the engine burned up. The oil light was on, and the car just stopped. We've been real blessed to catch rides this far. The last one dropped us off in south Jackson. Since it started raining, I haven't seen anyone even slow down until you came along."

Marshall said, "We'll stop at McDonald's and think about what to do. I need to make a couple of phone calls."

Making their stop, the three wayfarers headed for the restroom while Marshall checked his money and ordered happy meals for the threesome. Looking better or at least drier, the three were soon seated and waiting. As they occupied themselves with the food and milk with coffee for the mother, Marshall headed for the bank of telephones. First the babysitter to let her know of the delay, then a call to one of his carpet-cleaning patrons.

He had contracts with several apartment managers for clean-outs after people moved out. Their referrals had led to periodic cleaning in several hotels. Soon he had made arrangements.

He picked up his cup of coffee and joined the happy group. "Y'all will be staying at the Jacksonian tonight. Your breakfast will be waiting for you at Lefleur's, just across from the hotel."

After he ushered the three inside, and Susan had the room key, he dug into his wallet and handed her ten dollars. "I don't have the money for a bus, but this will get you lunch maybe."

"I don't know when I'll be able to pay you back," she started.

"I've been in situations where I needed help. Sometimes I got it, and sometimes I didn't. You can pay me back when you settle in and are on your feet.

"Just do something for someone else."

BIG HEART, TOO

Dot Day

The next days were still messy and cold. Marshall returned to the Jacksonian the following day where he found the little group had eaten their breakfasts and checked out. He set out along the frontage road looking for them. After several miles he gave up.

Guess they got a ride after all.

The phone rang often at the shop that day with customers rescheduling their cleaning. He answered them instead of letting the answering service take the messages. By that afternoon, he was stir-crazy. Marshall busied himself with cleaning the shop and office area. The van would be next.

The phone rang again. He had not turned it over to be answered yet. "AAA Carpet Cleaning," he answered.

"Bill Clark here. Do you, by any chance, clean carpets in cars? I have some mud in mine. We have a family trip coming up this weekend, and I want it clean."

"I don't usually, but I'll be cleaning mine, so bring yours on down to my shop." He gave directions and resumed his cleaning.

The tall man, casually dressed in slacks and sweater, drove his Lincoln on into the shop. "It's a fair bit of mud, some not yet dried. Think you can get it clean?"

Marshall continued uncoiling the hose. "Look at the van. I had some muddy passengers; bet you can't tell it now."

Bill whistled. "Sharp."

"Thanks — not too bad when you have the right equipment. I picked up a small family yesterday hitchhiking in that stew of mud and rain."

"Was it a woman named Susan with a boy and girl with her?"

"Yes. Did you know them? I picked them up Wednesday and helped them find a place to stay. I went back looking for them and missed them by an hour. I hope they made it to Memphis."

Bill laughed. "It turns out they were going to Little Rock, not Memphis. I saw them at the Madison exit ramp. Couldn't stand the idea of children being out in that mess. So, I offered them a ride and breakfast."

"Were they hungry?"

"No, the kids sang the praises of the man who let them stay in his hotel and paid for their breakfast. John Mark said he was going to be like him when he grew up. I'm guessing that was you."

Marshall colored as he chuckled at the thought of 'his' hotel. "Yeah, I took them to 'my' hotel. It is mine as far as the carpets get steam-cleaned regularly, and I'm the cleaning man. But, tell me, how far did you get them? I wonder why she told me Memphis and you Little Rock."

"They had been on the road long enough to get their shoes and bags muddy again. I called my wife. She told me to bring 'em to the house and we'd see what we could do about getting them on home. She outfitted them, washed their clothes.

"I listened to Susan's story. She left a bad situation with a sorry wife-beater husband. When I told her we would work to get her bus tickets, she changed her story from Memphis to Little Rock. I called the church and they agreed to collect the money. So, I got a few others to pitch in. By the time their clothes and shoes

Ordinary Miracles

finished in the dryer, we had the full amount promised. My wife and I loaded them on the bus."

"Pleased to know you, Bill Clark. There aren't many men who would stop in that mess, particularly in a Lincoln. This cleaning is on me."

"Likewise, I'm pleased to meet you. I'll take the free cleaning if you'll take my tip for it."

Two men with big hearts shook hands.

Editor's Note: I had heard these two stories from my brother and recreated them. Because Bill Clark was a player in this soggy drama, I sent them on to him. He suggested modifications, something about a slim, good-looking suave man tooling along Interstate 55 with the Mississippi Department of Transportation still working on the shoulders. He was driving along in his new GMC Buccaneer 1978 model van with a television antenna and broadcasting paraphernalia on top. He and younger daughter Kim regularly took his older daughter Christie to school. The duo was headed north near Blackwell Chevrolet.

Kim, standing between the bucket seats spotted them first. They appeared to be two adults with a little girl. Her question to her dad was a stimulus to action. "Daddy, what do you think will happen to them?" Actually, it was a mid-teens young man escorting his sister and niece as they made their way to Louisville, Kentucky. The rest of the story played out as noted.

ADDENDUM, BIG HEART

Bill Clark
Edited by Barbara Gaddy

It's hard to know where to start with this character, my wonderful friend of over 45 years — Robert Reynolds. Born with cerebral palsy, he was raised by a loving grandmother on the Gold Coast in Rankin County.

When I first met him back in the '70s, he was delivering shoes for Smith City Shoe Shop. He could be spotted all over town aboard his familiar three-wheel bike. Then, he was hired during the William Winter Administration as a runner for the state of Mississippi ... delivering important state business from department to department, rain or shine, tooling around in a Cushman.

If someone needed an appointment with the Governor, they just followed Robert. He could and would walk in unannounced.

Following are a few special "Robert memories."

1/18/2016

Robert Reynolds will be 71 years old this Friday, January 22. Only wish I had space here to tell about the many life experiences and events we have shared, both joyful and not so joyful. I once read that people come into our lives for A Reason, A Season, or

A Lifetime. Robert is one of those Lifetimers. Despite physical challenges from birth, his tenacity, dogged determination, and never-give-up-spirit have been an inspiration to everyone he has touched along the highway of life. From my entire family, Robert, thank you for being one of us. See Ya Friday, old dude!

1/22/2017

We have been tight well over 40 years now. Too many fun (and a few sad) times to pass along in a Facebook post, although I'll touch on a few. Many of you around the Jackson area will remember him; his eminence — Sir Robert Reynolds.

Today (1/22/17) is his 72nd birthday, and it was time to break out the cupcakes.

He is a remarkable individual and someone who has inspired me since the first day we met. He accepted me as I was, and I returned the sentiment.

Robert was born with cerebral palsy, and some would say, on the wrong side of the tracks. Overwhelmed, his young mother relegated his upbringing to her parents. They did something right!

When we met, Robert was working for a shoe shop delivering shoes all over town pedaling a three-wheeler. Hot weather, icy cold, or in the rain, he was making his rounds.

Years ago (1978), I had a phone conversation with a prominent banker about Robert, and when he found out he and I were friends he said, "Any friend of Robert's is a friend of mine." It was a Lucky Day, because with Frank's help, along with a cadre of other kindred spirits/volunteers, we were able to move Robert and his grandfather from a dilapidated old house on what was then called The Gold Coast into a fully remodeled, completely furnished little WWII vintage house in a better area of town. His grandfather died just a couple of years after moving into the new house, but Robert lived there another 30+ years until he moved into a nursing home a few years ago where he lives now.

He retired from the State of Mississippi where he later worked delivering mail and packages to various state agencies. Robert invited me to join in the festivities when Governor Fordice named him Mississippi's Employee of the Year. When he retired during the Musgrove administration, I got to 'splain (one might say roast) him a bit at his well-earned reception.

Robert is my friend with friends in high places; not to name drop, but the late Mary Ann Mobley and Gary Collins were his buds, for example. They once flew him to California for a few days R & R with them.

For years, until he was no longer able to get out and about as much, he would spend Thanksgiving and Christmas with the Clarks and Carrs, not as a guest, but as a member of our families. My wife and three daughters love him as much as I do. My sister and brother-in-law, Martha and James Carr, as well.

He and I still stay in close contact, although he has to bear with me and repeat things while I try to interpret his unique and increasingly thick brand of southern drawl. Thankfully, he is a patient man.

I would be remiss not to thank (on Robert's behalf) all the great FORs (friends of Robert's) who through the years have helped make this Jackson Icon's life more livable and enjoyable. A special shout-out goes to Pat Smith, executive director of The Lucky Day Foundation. WOW! You are "The Best," Pat!

If I ever write a book, Robert will be the focus of the longest chapter. I love the guy!

Happy birthday, my Supercalifragilisticexpialidocious friend.

Dorothy A. Day

12/25/2018

Precious few of us don't have a need for friends in high places from time-to-time. One of my go-to guys in such situations has always been my long-time great friend, the esteemed Mr. Robert Reynolds. Although Robert has dealt with the disability of cerebral palsy and impaired speech since birth, that hasn't kept him from making a serious contribution to our community and being an inspiration to all who cross his path.

We first met over 40 years ago when he was with Smith City Shoe Shop just west of the viaduct on Capitol Street. Come rain or shine, cold or heat, Robert pedaled all over town delivering expertly repaired shoes to Jackson's movers and shakers on a three-wheel bicycle. He kept Jacksonians "lookin' good."

During the William Winter administration, he joined the State of Mississippi in communications. Well, kinda/sorta. He delivered the important work of the state to various state agencies as a runner — this time, however, he tooled around in a fancy three-wheel Cushman with a nifty cab that kept him out of the rain. That little puppy (several of them, in fact) also had a heater for those cold winter days. The benefactor, who would never have wanted his generosity made public during his lifetime, was none other than Frank Day, Chairman of Trustmark Bank. Through Robert, I met Frank. He and I conspired together to the benefit of Robert on other important projects including a house. Frank furnished the funds and I (and other Robert friends), the sweat.

Robert was great friends with Mary Ann Mobley and Gary Collins. Again, I met them through Mr. Big — Robert Reynolds.

A few years later when he retired from his state job (with all the heavies in attendance), I got to tell his story and roast him. The roasting wasn't pretty!

For a number of years, he lived at Chadwick Nursing and Rehabilitation Center on Chadwick Drive. He still calls two/three times a week just to check on me, and though he is hard to understand, I know he is checking to see that I am toeing the line.

I dearly love the guy, and he will often call and express that sentiment in return. There simply isn't room in this format to tell all my "Reynolds" stories. Look for them in my book. I have finished numbering the pages.

Merry Christmas, my friend — and thanks for your friendship, your love, and for your contribution toward making our state a better place to live. Robert Reynolds — a guy whose very personality personifies Mississippi's monicker as the — "Hospitality State."

Postlude: I wrote this post sitting in my vehicle before leaving Chadwick. I went back in and read him the post. He was so excited! I read some of the early comments to him. I'll visit him again soon and read him more. Thanks to each of you for brightening his day.

1/22/2019

And what a party it was — Robert Reynold's 74th. The folks at Martin's Restaurant on South State Street rolled out the red carpet for this (back-in-the-day) longtime-iconic special customer.

Joining us were a couple of Robert's friends from his growing-up years; Allen Stephens and Joe Bradshaw. Jesse Houston made a surprise visit in his wheelchair — made possible by Paul and Jackie Early, owner of Dickey's Barbecue Restaurants in the metro. Jackie is Jesse's sister. My sister, Martha Carr, a longtime friend of Robert's as well, furnished the cupcakes.

Afterwards, Robert and I rode through downtown Jackson, pausing briefly along the street to speak with local attorney and judge, Bob Waller. Robert was/is one of those fellows who knew everybody, and everybody knew him.

As I am writing this I can just see and hear Robert blowing (a squeeze type) the horn on his three-wheel bike in a parade ... or when he would see a friend on the street. Seems times were less complicated then — more Norman Rockwell-ish.

Happy Birthday, Robert Reynolds. Let's get another birthday in the books and do it again next year my friend!

12/9/2019

Monday, December 9, marks the fifth anniversary of the passing of Mary Ann Mobley Collins, one of Mississippi's most beloved daughters and ambassadors. It's yet another reminder of just how fast time passes.

I did not know Mary Ann personally and had never met her. However, she and Gary befriended our mutual friend (and Mary Ann's fellow Rankin County long-time friend), Robert Reynolds. Gary and I spoke regarding Robert occasionally, and he sent money a couple of times for Robert's birthday or Christmas. They flew him to California for a visit with them many years ago. My connection with them was through Robert, our mutual buddy.

Beginning just a few weeks before her death (cancer), Robert began insisting I phone her. He told me she knew me through him and said he wouldn't be satisfied until she and I had a conversation. While I was reluctant to call her, at Robert's unrelenting insistence, I did so. Turns out, she and I had a wonderful conversation — with her expressing genuine thanks for the call. What??? Her thanking me???

We expressed our mutual awe and appreciation of Robert and the way in which he has successfully dealt with the life-long challenge of severe cerebral palsy.

I told her that I had been on Mary Ann Drive in Brandon just the day before. She asked if I had stopped to clean the signs (there are several, in fact). I confessed that I had not, but that I would keep an eye on them. I do. Just today (Sunday, December 8th) I checked them out. They looked to be in great condition.

Ordinary Miracles

Following her death at home in Los Angeles just a couple of weeks following our conversation, the minister at Christ United Methodist Church in Jackson, Mississippi, said Mary Ann had wanted a bench placed near her grave in the hope that folks would stop by and visit with her. I have done so a couple of times as I have been in the cemetery for other burials. I just may go tomorrow on the 5th anniversary of the death of one of Mississippi's most beloved daughters, good-will ambassadors, and notable personalities.

It's interesting that one of her street signs shares the pole with another distinguished personality from Brandon, Mississippi — former Commandant of the Marine Corps and Congressional Medal of Honor recipient, Four Star General Lewis H. Wilson. Go figure!

12/25/2019

My friend, Robert Reynolds, wanted me to wish everyone a very Merry Christmas today — Christmas 2019. However, he wasn't spruced up and didn't want me to post his picture from today. I am happy to say that he is still doing relatively well.

For those who aren't familiar with him, he is an amazing fellow and one of my very long-time friends. Should anyone wish to phone him please private message me for his phone number. He would be delighted to hear from you. Don't be concerned that he is difficult to understand. Both of you will still get the message. Again, Merry Christmas from THE Man — Esquire Robert Reynolds.

During the Fordice Administration, he was selected outstanding state employee of the year. He asked me to join him for the presentation. When he retired during the Musgrove administration, he asked me to join him again for his retirement reception. I roasted him fittingly. I'm not sure he has ever forgiven me.

Upon finding out Robert was my close friend, the late Frank "Brum" Day (one time top-of-heap at Trustmark Bank) told me, "Any friend of Robert's is a friend of mine." Frank and I conspired to buy Robert a house. I agreed to use Frank's money. Ha! Then, I, along with the sweat of 25-30 of my closest friends, remodeled that little house and turned it into a cozy cottage. Such fun! Such memories!

At Robert's insistence, I spoke with the late Mary Ann Mobley (Mississippi's first Miss America) two weeks before her death. He and Mary Ann were life-long friends and he insisted I phone her on his behalf (at her California home) to check on her. She was thrilled to hear from him even via proxy. That call made the day for all three of us.

With so many people having known Robert through the years, I like to give an update on him from time to time. A friend had given me a fancy chair, but Mrs. Clark said we didn't have a place for it. I knew who might, so I re-gifted it. Robert was ecstatic and enjoyed it while at Chadwick Nursing Home! Whenever one visited Robert at Chadwick's, he always left feeling really good.

10/30/2021

It is with considerable sadness blended with a slight hint of joy (given his declined condition) to post that Robert Reynolds passed away this morning, Saturday, October 30. He is no longer a prisoner to a twisted body, an awkward walk, slurred speech, and more recently … failing health. Born with cerebral palsy to a single mom, who wasn't emotionally equipped to deal with him, Robert was raised by his grandparents.

There is absolutely no doubt God put him in my pathway almost 50 years ago. As a result of our having met, it became my high honor to become his brother-from-another-mother and go-to guy.

When Robert and I met, he was working at Smith City Shoe Shop delivering repaired, refurbished, and shined shoes to a vibrant and dynamic downtown community of Jackson's movers and shakers. Robert knew everybody and everybody knew him.

Word is that he could/would walk into the Governor's office unannounced; the business of State would be tabled during his visit. I would hear the same occurred in the executive suite at First National Bank (now Trustmark) according to Trust'ed sources.

Robert retired from the State of Mississippi where he was employed as a runner. I called him the state communications director because he delivered mail, intra-office communication and packages that kept the rails of state business greased and functioning. Robert was recognized as the State of Mississippi's employee of the year during the Fordice administration. He asked me to attend the award presentation as his guest. Of course, I did!

The Facebook venue (and time) doesn't allow me the space/freedom to relay my many Robert stories. I'll try to reduce those to remarks I will deliver at his funeral. Possibly I can post them if Facebook will allow me enough digits.

His passing certainly leaves quite a void in my life and others. On behalf of Robert, I wish to especially thank Pat Smith, administrator of The Lucky Day Foundation, for her incredible life's walk with Robert in overseeing his finances AND for being an ear, a confidante, and a facilitator on his behalf. Also, in more recent years, Dot Porter, who has a sister at Chadwick and whose husband is Robert's distant relative, was one of Robert's angels. Dot has been awesome as Robert's liaison to and with Chadwick Nursing and Rehabilitation Center where he has been a resident for a number of years.

My daughters, Christi, Kim, and Julie, adored Robert. My wife Jean and sister Martha did as well. My thanks to them for unequivocally including Robert in our family gatherings and for treating him with the love and respect he deserved as our dear extended family member.

Many years ago Robert asked me if I would sing at his funeral. I now wish I had said … "maybe." WOW!

Robert's life has been quite a ride — literally; much of it on a two-wheel bicycle, then a three-wheel bicycle, and several three-wheel motorized Cushmans, made possible by the generosity of the late Frank Day.

Then there was that 'lil refurbished WWII style house Robert and his grandfather relocated to in 1978 (again) thanks to the generosity of Frank Day and the sweat and elbow grease of volunteer angels at First Baptist Church, Madison, and many others. To have been the instigator/facilitator/coordinator of that effort remains one of the great joys of my life.

Condolences to sons Matt (wife Memory), Carl and Daniel.

Robert Reynolds. January 22, 1945 – October 30, 2021.
Love 'ya, Brother!

11/17/2021

On Wednesday, one week ago today, we buried this amazing fellow and my dear friend — Robert Reynolds. I'll miss him immensely.

Cerebral Palsy never seemed to dampen Robert's spirit. From time-to-time he would tell me (in his severely slurred speech) how he wished he could talk. I would tell him he wouldn't be Robert if he could talk.

On a few occasions throughout our 40-plus year friendship (when I couldn't understand a word he was saying and couldn't get him to stop talking) I would lay down the phone and go on about my business. To be brutally honest, I have hung up on him a time or two.

The Bible says, "Inasmuch as you have done it unto the least of these, My brethren, you have done unto me." That I may have hung up on Jesus has me more than a little concerned. Yikes! Anyway, we would quickly reconnect with my point having been made. I genuinely loved Robert and he loved me — at least he said he did. Ha!

SO many Robert stories I could tell. Some hilarious — some sad — none mundane.

When God first put Robert in my path, approaching fifty years ago, he was delivering shoes on a three-wheel bicycle for Smith City Shoe Shop. He had a large and LOUD squeeze-type horn on the handlebar — which he used frequently when he saw friends on the street or otherwise wanted to make his presence known. In my minds-eye, I can picture Robert on his three-wheel bicycle honking that horn, and it brings back such fun Norman Rockwell-ish memories from another time and place.

Later, when Robert went to work for the state of Mississippi as a courier, he (through the ongoing generosity of a Jackson banker) upgraded his Ride to Cushmans. God bless the late banker.

At his funeral last Wednesday, it just seemed fitting to me that us FORs (friends of Robert's) "Honk" him out of the funeral home chapel and into the hearse. It's virtually impossible to Honk a squeeze horn and not smile ... so we did! Laughed too! Robert Reynolds would have loved each and every honk!

Special thanks to Dr. Jerry File, Candylee Dobbs Jones, and Paul Earley for honoring Robert by their contribution to the service; and to Matt Reynolds, who delivered a moving tribute to his father.

Through nothing short of a miracle, Robert has been laid to rest in a beautiful country church cemetery in Yazoo County immediately next to his grandparents and his mother.

5/10/2022

On Saturday, the day before my significant birthday (they all are) this Mother's Day, I spent some time foraging through old photo boxes. Well, lo and behold … there was my buddy, Esquire Robert Reynolds, pictured with former Governor Kirk Fordice. The occasion was Robert being named the State of Mississippi's employee of the year for the year 1993. Reynolds, as I called him, had asked me to accompany him.

Officially, Robert worked in the mail room as a runner, delivering mail and other secrets-of-state amongst the bureaucrats. Functionally, I considered him to be the Director of Communications and Hospitality Director for the State of Mississippi.

As many of you know, Robert passed away at the age of 76 on October 30, 2021, at Chadwick Nursing and Rehabilitation Center. Robert was one of those amazing iconic guys who only comes along once every eternity or so.

Honk on, dear friend — and don't ride the clutch too much. Maintenance may give you a really hard time on that lifetime warranty.

1/22/2023

Today (01/22/23) would have been my friend Robert Reynold's 78th birthday. He and I crossed paths in the late 60's; what a ride the friendship became. A people-person, being confined to a small room at Chadwick Nursing and Rehabilitation Center was quite challenging for him during the last years of his life. The Covid years compounded the challenge. Somehow, he managed. That he did is a testament to the human spirit. Rest in peace, dear friend.

EZEKIEL SAW THE WHEEL
Averyell Kessler

I love gospel music, always have. I've worn out two Mississippi Mass Choir CD's as well as one from The Gospel at Newport, an album recorded at the Newport Jazz Festival in the late 1950s.

I began listening to it years ago because of its joyous message, bright harmony and simple, haunting melodies. It's an easy listen, no training required. It's the gospel straight on without the heavy burden of theology. Gospel music is an explosion of joyous belief, no questions asked. Thees and thous are excluded, as well as the mental gymnastics required to produce a logical (aka human) explanation of faith.

My first taste of gospel music came from the glorious alto voice of our housekeeper Ella Mason as she sang "Swing Low, Sweet Chariot." It also blared from a Westinghouse radio perched on the window ledge in Mama's kitchen. "Deep River" was often interspersed between Rinso Blue commercials and Farmer Jim Neal. Later, I learned that Elvis, the king of Rock'n Roll, was also a big fan of gospel music, "There'll Be Peace in the Valley" among them.

One of my favorites is "Ezekiel Saw the Wheel." In gospel music, the name is pronounced E-zee-kell. For me, it's a succinct explanation of my simplistic beliefs as a Christian, without any attempt to slither around the basics of the gospel.

Dorothy A. Day

So, here's a bit of heresy if you'd like to call it that. I'm sorry that theology came along. I say this with all due respect for those who are heavily invested and after I finished a four-year course of home study from a respected divinity school, not once but twice.

It was an enlightening study and with an overflow of benefits. However, somewhere along the way, I realized that theology is merely an education in human thought. It's a futile attempt to figure everything out and adopt a logical version of religion that makes sense to a scholar's enlightened mind.

When I realized that just wasn't possible, I felt as if I'd shrugged off a heavy winter coat. The overwhelming power of God's love makes no sense; his astounding gift of Jesus makes no sense. Nor does the resurrection, or Jesus' amazing promise to raise us up. It is not, as some think, the result of a strict interpretation of scripture or its proper translation.

It is, also, not a pale and palatable version of God that pleases careful, modern sensibilities. As much as I'd like to purchase a non-refundable ticket to Heaven and slip it into my pocket, that's not possible either. It's God's gift. There is no complicated contract or a cumbersome list of conditions and requirements. Only two, love God with all your heart, and your neighbor as yourself.

More and more, it seems as if folks are looking for a human explanation of the gospel, one that fits snugly into a highly educated brain. Why do we seek an answer in the inexplicable and push back against an upside-down, inside-out, not-like-it's-supposed-to-be rejection of human reason?

The totality of tangled explanations, educated guesses, laws of nature and life experience is thrown out of the window. Jesus' words are so simple; our attempts to shape them so futile. Why tamper with His glorious statement, "*I shall lose nothing of all that he has given me but raise it up at the last day.*" I shall lose nothing! What a wonderful promise.

Ordinary Miracles

My buddy Ezekiel, prophet of God, saw the wheels way up in the middle of the air, the little wheel run by faith, the big wheel run by the grace of God. Thankfully, people are still singing about those wheels. I'm aware that there are multiple explanations of Ezekiel's vision and what some folks think it means; but in the end, God is running his big grace wheel without any help from us. No explanation needed. It is his glorious and loving gift. The little wheel, faith, is propelled only by his grace. *Anyone who desires, may take the water of life without price.* For me, that sums it all up.

Easter is only a few days away. One like I've never experienced. One I hope I'll never see again. But it can't be stopped, no matter what occurs in the world, not by isolation, worry or stress; not by hardship, war, discord, or fear. Best of all, it can't be stopped by disease. So, rejoice.

Weeping may last for a night, but joy comes in the morning.
Psalm 30:5

BEHIND THE GARAGE
Averyell Kessler

Jackson, Mississippi, 1959

I learned a lot about life behind the garage. Deep, dark and oily, it was a place of intrigue.

Our garage was a typical two-car wooden behemoth, nesting behind our Laurel Street home and a good fifteen yards from our back door. Spare bicycle chains and clothesline rope hung from the walls, as well as a tin wash tub, a collection of rakes and saws, and a display of license plates from the last seven years. We had only one car, a black Chevy sedan, so the vacant space was used for rainy day roller skating, hopscotch and storing Daddy's push lawn mower and wheelbarrow.

But behind it, a secret garden!

It was only a narrow patch of grass between the back wall of the garage and our neighbors' fence. Not a thing like Mary and Colin's lovely hideaway, but to me, it was a private sanctuary, a childhood nirvana, free from adult eyes. My friend Martha and I found it early on and made it our clubhouse — no grown-ups allowed! She was seven, I was six.

Martha had an older brother and knew the ways of the world, I was an only child and needed advice. She taught me the difference between gold and white honeysuckle and how to bite off the tips and suck out its sweet juice. I learned how to survive my first day at school, step around rowdy boys and avoid slimy mounds of spinach in the cafeteria. Together we spit watermelon seeds, dug up roly polys, and captured ladybugs in mason jars. We watched tree frogs and ruby-throated lizards, touched spider webs glistening with dew and saw grasshoppers lolling in the sun. Happily, no snakes! Before summer ended, we learned about heat lightening, made kites out of sticks and newspaper, and recognized the earthy smell of rain falling on dirt.

Our hideout was also a place for serious discussions, to work out our childhood theology, question how Noah got all those animals onto the ark, and ask why some people thought boys were wonderful, when we both knew they were loud and disgusting. Although the subject of babies never came up, we dismissed outright the idea that a stork dropped us off. "Something happens," Martha whispered. "My brother knows, but he won't tell."

We moved when I was twelve, and I've never been back to the Laurel Street house. I wonder if my secret garden is still there, if that sweet place of gentle silence survives, and little girls are telling secrets in the soft summer heat. I hope that every so often, children will step outside to catch bugs and taste honeysuckle. Maybe they'll run through the sprinkler or wave sparklers in the midnight sky. I want them to search for four-leaf clovers in the yard, blow bubbles, eat grape popsicles, and let mud ooze between their toes. I hope they'll rake seeds out of watermelons and spit them over the back fence. Most of all, I wish they'll hide behind the garage and try to figure things out.

FALL #47

Dot A. Day

Three-thirty a.m., I am fully awake.

I rouse Charles to help me from the bed into my wheelchair to make my way to the bathroom. Rolling the chair to a point perpendicular to the commode, I get onto the toilet without help. No problem until I begin the return to my chair.

Semi-independent, I stand to begin to get into my chair. Right foot is firmly on the floor, and the right calf presses against the footrest of the power wheelchair. Likewise, the left foot is in full contact with the floor and the left thigh rests against the ringed seat of the commode. The mantra of the physical therapist is followed: *Foot on the floor and nose over toes.*

My left foot tendon is loose because of surgery. Sometimes my foot is uncooperative, and I have my weight on the turned-over ankle and outer side of my foot. The right and left hands firmly grasp the armrests of the wheelchair and then the handles of the hydraulic lift seat of the commode. I lean my torso forward to begin to turn my left foot to the left, and the right one to follow a similar pattern.

All movements are slow and thought out. Suddenly, the right leg buckles and my knee gives way. My grip is not strong enough to keep me up.

I fall face first, hitting a small wash pan and sounding my personal scream of alarm. The pan is large enough to cause me to rotate my body so that I end up lying supine. My head is tightly bound by the shower wall. *Thank you, Lord; two more inches and I probably would've broken my neck.* I am grateful the pan is here so that I don't fall on my face. This part happened in less than a minute.

Charles has rushed to help me, and he and I take inventory. So far, there are bumps, and there will be bruises. He grasps my ankles pulling me forward to alleviate the pressure on my head and neck. He teepees my legs so I don't have pressure on my back.

I wait, impatient, frustrated, as he goes to the garage to get the Hoyer lift. Then he pulls my body through the shower area lengthwise to align me to use the lift. Between the two of us, we remember enough of the instructions for him to get me into the sling and to lift me hydraulically into the swing device and lower me into my chair. Further inventory reveals a pulled groin muscle. This part probably took forty-five minutes. I stay up the remainder of the night.

Charles has stayed close today, picking me up for transfers for toileting and bed. My sense of control is nonexistent. I desire to feel or to be in control, but it will not happen.

At 10 p.m., bedtime, I sit on the edge of the bed with Charles's help in transferring from the power wheelchair. He swings my legs up onto the mattress as I lie back. "Are you okay; do you need to move?"

I agree all is okay, and he turns off the light. Physically I am okay, but my emotions, not so much.

I take another inventory. My emotions start screaming, and there is no gratitude. *It's too soon. I can't give up. I won't give up.* I become very aware of my body and my breathing. It's not my body. It's too tight, too constricting. I don't fit.

My head is too far down in the bed. My feet are too tight against the foam wedge that keeps the weight of the covers from my feet. Similar to my experience in the shower, there's not enough room, and I am jammed up in the bed.

I can't breathe. I am drowning in shallow breaths. Mind over matter. Breathe ... breathe through your nose and hold it. Get it circulating down and down in the diaphragm. Are you going to have a panic attack? Get yourself under control.

I become aware that I have no control. I can't move; I can't turn over. I can't reach out for a drink of water. If there were to be an emergency, I couldn't reach the phone to call 911. I'm dependent. Almost totally dependent. Soon I will be worse than now. What if I couldn't speak, if my diaphragm muscles couldn't make the effort?

I use the thumb on my right hand to find the control and raise the head of the mattress to a 45° angle. I'm still struggling; my feet are too tight against the foam pillow. I am in the bed, and there is not enough room for me.

"Charles I've got to get up. I've got to sit up tonight."

"You need your rest ... Just lie here and go to sleep ... Relax."

He is going to make me lie here. Dizzy now ... I can't breathe. My breaths are small and jagged, not deep enough despite my coaching.

"Please get me back up. I can't breathe. I'll be fine sitting up."

He reverses the getting into bed actions. I begin to get a sense of control as I return to the living room. I read for a short while, and then I fall asleep, sitting in a reclined position in the power wheelchair.

Author's Note: Indeed the shallow breathing became a problem the doctor addressed by ordering a noninvasive ventilator. My oxygen level at night hovered around fifty percent prior to its use. I really couldn't breathe.

NARRATIVE

Lauren E. Harris

A busted lock. The wooden cellar door swings open. Cobwebs fly as a fresh gust of air propels them further into the deepest depths of this ancient tomb. The gust of wind swirls as the stale air fuses with the fresh breeze. But in an instant, almost like magic, the tornado dissipates into nothingness as it reaches into the shadowed corner of the room.

I hesitate to follow it. but follow it I did. Looking back at it now, that single moment captures one of the stupidest yet most brilliant choices of my life. Yet it wasn't a choice, more of an inner trance, a moment of hypnosis, so to speak. Yet, it seemed for naught as the mystery seemed over.

Just an empty corner. Well, not completely empty. A strange book lay closed on the cement. I obviously had to pick the book up, but it wouldn't budge. Even stranger, there was no title nor author. Everything was unknown. My fingers grazed the worn leather; turning the page, a burst of golden light suddenly illuminated the room. Once again, I heard and followed the angelic calling as I dove into the book.

Awakening, I saw a marbled ceiling ornately decorated with golden molding that seemed to be shelving books. As I arose from the floor, my senses became in tune with my surroundings. No doors, no windows, only books! Every surface was covered with books. A library, a very beloved library indeed. In the center of it all, a desk. Oddly, there was no chair, no furniture, but only a desk. On that desk, a note reading, "When it is time to write, it will appear."

I only thought I was confused before when I was sucked in here, but, oh, was I wrong? What will appear? Write what? How do I leave? Honestly, I didn't think about that until many hours later. How do I know it was many hours later, I do not know. But my personal indicator happened to be my stomach.

I lay on the floor for hours, now bored out of my mind. Some would ask why when I have all these books, but based on my last encounter, can you really blame me? A flash. I dashed to the desk as my inner squabbles were interrupted for a short period of time until I actually read the note.

"You cannot write what you do not know. KNOW."

Personally, that last note was maddeningly unhelpful. I pondered for several more hours. What in the world was I supposed to know? Well, this is a library, so I guess I must once again open a book to find out.

I begin my search at the corner then work my way to the right. That way, when I'm lost in this overwhelming sea of books, I have a system to find my way out, if there is even an out. Something flickered and caught my eye. A nameplate! Maybe if there was a name, I could figure out who was behind all this chaos.

Yet, the tag only read "Curiosity leads to knowing, The Author." I just thought the other was unhelpful; this one was just downright confusing. All in all, I gave in and picked up a book from the top shelf. As nervous as I was, I threw caution to the wind. My boredom left no other option but to read. As I caved and opened the book ...."

Did y'all actually think that I would share that easily? No, you must seek to **KNOW**, but I will say, I've had many of the greatest

Ordinary Miracles

adventures one could imagine. Others were so unimaginable I wouldn't know where to start in my description. All I know is all I know. **KNOW.**

A rush of understanding and sadness overcame Max as she put the final book on the shelf. Her paradise would pass on to another; her tales would live on for the next to read. But, not just read — explore. The back wall.

The back wall held her favorite books, well, more like a sea captain's journals. Each traveler had shared his deepest thoughts with her as she too made the journey. No, they were not just travelers; they were her dearest friends and companions. Max glided across the oak floors, floors where she had spent hours dancing with princes and fighting pirates, grazing the spines of her beloved books. What she would do to feel that electric shock rush through her veins just once more. Max returned to her desk once more to write but not a book; her own set of secret clues she would leave behind for the next. She understood now. She knew now.

Max hesitantly walked to the center of the once-vibrant golden room that had dimmed with age and opened the book that started it all. Only one last goodbye would be said. The stale air scented by beloved books swirled once more. Max awakened on a lounge and above her, not a ceiling, but a sea of faces. Her beloved comrades greet her as she has become The Author of her own story.

Max not only knew but she **TOLD.**

LOVE OF THE GAME
Dot Day

You stand there, watching, planning, managing.
The Bill's-Batteries blues take the field.
You stretch your legs, warming up to run.
Like a motor revving up to full throttle, it's " Play ball."
The action starts. "Batter up" —
Words remind to focus, plant feet in balance as you pick
your spot.
Right, left, center?
No, line drive over first.
The old-style uniform — yellow leggings, blue-sleeves
under the team tee sheathe latent desire.
I wish you had fulfilled the dream fueled by a six-year-old
competing in the league with those ranging in age to twelve.
But, like an anxious beaver, I gnaw:
"Would you have been in my life?
Might we not have met?"
Deliberate, disciplined, devoted motions of play,
You foster love for a game.
You astonish me with your easy grace,
How you dive to catch a ball, flipping over end to
Rebound and throw out the runner who left without tagging.

Dorothy A. Day

The harsh yellow rays darken your face under its
brimmed blue cap,
And the scent of metallic bats and old leather override
the salty sweat.
Like a surveyor evaluating his elevation,
you choose the spot to get a hit to advance your runner.
Over third, line drive.
It's a life spent in play and in love for a game;
Then the tier of lights flickers out.
The game is done and won.

LULA'S MEMORIES OF CHILDHOOD

Dot Barker

The weather was dismal as the clouds hung low in the sky waiting for the rain to come pounding down on the rooftop. The weather seems to be a very good excuse to stay inside and look at the empty house hoping to find something to fill the morning.

My eyes fell on the photo album filled with family pictures from our childhood. I opened the album to stare at the stern face of my grandmother. She usually had an amazing story about anyone in the family, especially a good scandal from the past. My grandmother believed everyone had a secret hidden away in his or her closet just waiting to come out as a good scandalous story.

I could close my eyes and see the ten-year-old girl sitting at my grandmother's feet waiting for the next tale of long ago. "Tell me about when you were a little girl," I begged.

A slight smile crossed the wrinkled face as she rubbed her hand over the worn cover of the Bible lying in her lap.

"First, I have to tell you about Poppa and Momma and how they met because without them I wouldn't be here to tell the story.

"Poppa was a plantation owner up in Attala County and was married to Miss Nellie. Miss Nellie's parents were well-to-do people. Poppa and Miss Nellie had four children, two boys and two girls. Momma's family worked on Poppa's plantation several years. Momma worked for Miss Nellie helping with the household chores and the children. About three years later, Miss Nellie got the fever and died. Poppa asked Momma to stay on and continue her duties.

"Poppa took a fancy to Momma, and later after a year or so she became the second Mrs. Owen Sanders. Momma's status took a turn she had never experienced, and really she didn't know how to handle being Mrs. Sanders and not a maid. Poppa explained she would now have help to take care of the house and the children, even though they were near adulthood. Even though Poppa was twenty-five years older than Momma, she thought she had found her Prince Charming.

"A year had passed when the babies started coming. First there was Lizzie, followed by Ornie, Maggie, Bill, Bell, then me (Lula) and finally baby Kate. After six girls don't know who was more exhausted, Momma or Poppa. If Poppa had decided on more children, there would have been more because he was master of the house, the field, his wife, and the children. You could hear a pin drop when Poppa spoke, no matter what the subject. We ate together, we went to church together, and nobody asked Poppa 'Why?' like children do today.

"The older children would play with us younger ones, but they always let us know they were Nellie's children and were special.

"Each morning we dressed, had breakfast, and went outside to play around the cedar trees leading up the path to the big sprawling two-story house with a large attic. This attic had caused me some pain because of a shining round box. What the box contained didn't really matter; I had to have the box. One morning as Poppa was finishing breakfast, I asked to be excused from the table. I found his coat, and in the pocket I found the shining round box. I hid the box in my apron pocket.

"When I finished my chores, I slipped up the stairs to the attic. When I was slightly hidden behind some boxes, I opened the box and found a dusty powder that looked like cocoa. I had seen Poppa put the dust in his lip, so I immediately did the same and found out if it was cocoa, it surely needed some sugar. Anything Poppa liked I would learn to like if it killed me. And it almost did.

"I kept the powder in my mouth until I started getting real sick. I tried to spit out the powder, but it had disappeared and just left me wanting to throw up my insides. I was found by my sisters when I didn't come to the table for dinner. Momma gave me some sassafras tea, and at that time it tasted good after swallowing all the brown powder. I was wishing I could die and never see the brown powder again. After my recovery Momma talked about misbehaving and switched my legs with a fine long limb from what was known as the 'switch bush.'

"The older children by Miss Nellie seemed to marry off about one a year. There was always a party following the wedding, but the younger children weren't included. We were marched up the stairs and into the bedrooms. The laughing and merrymaking were loud, but we knew we dare not go down the stairs. The house seemed a lot bigger after the older children were married and moved into their homes. The separation didn't seem to bother Miss Nellie's children because they visited only on holidays, and those visits were usually short.

"One morning right after my eighth birthday, Poppa had gone to the fields, and suddenly one of the hired hands came out and had Poppa on the back of the wagon. I remember he looked real pale, but Poppa was a giant in my eyes, so I figured he'd be all right. Someone went for the doctor. The doctor rushed to Poppa's bedroom. When he came out, he just shook his head and later that day Poppa died. We all were heartbroken, but for Momma the tears just wouldn't stop. The older children and their families came and

Poppa was buried. I didn't realize that my life was about to change forever.

"About three months after the funeral the two boys, Owen, Jr. and Frank, came by and called Momma into the parlor. As a curious child. I stood and listened outside the open door. Owen, Jr. was doing all the talking as he explained that everything Poppa owned now belonged to him and Frank and that Momma was welcome to live with us younger children in one of the sharecroppers' houses. Momma was a proud woman and declined the offer. The boys gave us a mule and small wagon to move our few belongings back to Leake County where our relatives now lived. Overnight Momma had come from being somebody special to being a woman with six small girls, no place to go, and nothing to do when she got to the end of the journey.

"The long driveway filled with dust. Six young girls sat in the back of the wagon and cried. We looked back at the big house that had been our home. Momma look straight ahead with her head high as she held the reins of the mule and moved into the main dirt road that would lead our family to Leake County and her family.

"I'm tired, so let's leave the rest of this journey for another day." My grandmother came to the end of the story as a sad look crossed a face that was worn with time and had experienced much hardship and joy in her years.

I picked the young girl off the floor from her grandmother's feet and closed the photo album on the many stories shared by my grandmother to me during my childhood.

THE DRESS
Dot Ainsworth Day

"Mom, we have our information for Vespers now. Heath will be lighting my candle." Stephanie smiled shyly as she shared this information. "We'll have to find a dress within two weeks."

It was break time at the rural private school where I taught foreign languages and English. Usually, we would be out in the cafeteria with the other students and teachers. However, I was giving a test the next period. I needed to make copies, then plan for my other class. Stephanie's request was not a surprise; however, unexpected surprises of a financial nature had depleted our budget. There was no money left for the discretionary purchase of a Vespers dress and not enough time or ability to make a suitable one. We would have to rent.

I put aside my lesson plan I had been working. My mind was fast at work, and I would need to choose my words carefully. Before I could tell her we needed to be frugal to make it to the end of the month, she spoke up. My sweet, introverted daughter showed herself thoughtful and sensitive.

"Mom, I don't have to take part. I know that's not much time to find a dress we can afford."

"Stephanie, you're right. But I'm trusting God to help us find the right dress." Her offer was precious, but I knew she wanted to be involved with her class.

Stephanie was a junior this year; Vespers is a ceremony near the end of school that passes candles as symbols of leadership from the seniors to the juniors. Probably it is the most beautiful of the various ceremonies and activities throughout the year. The young men wear tuxes, and the young women wear gowns — the fancy ones that a princess might wear with built up skirts and lace and sparkle, pastels for the juniors and white for the seniors.

At the end of the seniors' presentation, they begin exiting the stage dressed in white. Heath would light Stephanie's candle and go take his place on the balcony with the other seniors at the northern end of the gym. After each class sang a song, the seniors would extend their candles as if lighting those of the juniors. The juniors would respond by holding high their already-lighted candles. The seniors then extinguish their candles. Because I taught senior English and worked with the seniors, I relished their having one more night to shine before heading to a large university that would treat them as mere faces in a crowd.

I had been a religiously devout woman for many years. Around age 42, I realized I had come to God on my own, not at his calling. I wanted so much to belong to a group that I failed at the part of the "personal experience" that we Baptists claim is necessary to be born again. Then I had so much pride I couldn't accept I was lost. God got my full attention in Moses's story from Genesis 6-12. Several times Pharaoh hardened his heart; soon enough the passage reads, "God hardened Pharaoh's heart." Those words pushed me to honesty.

I would have a big faith test on waiting for God in this situation. I had already been praying about this. I knew that renting a dress was an option.

"Maybe we can find one to rent or check out 'Second-Hand Rose' for a consignment sale. If we go today, two weeks will be plenty of time for alteration or cleaning. I can't think of any other occasions where you might need a dress of this type. Do you mind renting it instead of purchasing or wearing one that has been used?"

"No, Mom, I agree. I know the money has been tight after buying Sharon's tires. It just makes sense not to buy it." Stephanie's face showed a subdued excitement.

I appreciated her sensitivity; Stephanie picks up intangible signals other young people most likely would not notice. Charles and I made a regular practice of explaining the need to stay within our budget limits. This dress would cause a strain; we usually had only enough money to last till the end of the month. I hooted at the idea of mad money; discretionary funds were unknown.

I was usually the perpetrator in testing the limits of the budget. I had difficulty telling myself "no" when it came to helping our daughters with their needs. Sharon was already in college at Mississippi State, working on campus, maintaining high honors grades, serving as a diamond girl. Yes, she had scholarships and student loans.

Like her sister, Stephanie was also busy. She had a job at a local gift shop, served as the captain of the flag squad, and was active with the student council. Neither one of the girls made demands, but my background of poverty left me with excessive pride, causing me to want to be conscientious about appearance, both mine and my family's. Those are not good combinations for someone at a private school. We paid our bills with the tithe coming out first, built our house with sweat equity, and paid off the credit card each month. We were greatly blessed and highly favored, responsible, and broke.

In the early 1990s, the terms 'online shopping' and 'Internet service' were not familiar, not even heard. At that time, one of our seniors had a new computer with the encyclopedia already installed. The computer class scheduled a special trip to his house just to see this latest desktop model; I think no one had a laptop at that point. So, Stephanie and I "let our fingers do the walking" through the Yellow Pages of the Jackson phonebook and lined up three possible stores.

Around 6 p.m. that evening, Stephanie and I had to admit defeat. We had made our way through rental places, consignment shops, and the Salvation Army store. Nothing. We sat in the parking lot. We had been hoping for a faith-building excursion that was not to be. We prayed again anyway and planned to make our way to Brookhaven over the weekend.

The next day my Spanish class trooped in. This class had three senior cheerleaders and Stephanie in it along with others. Whitney spoke up, "Senora, did y'all find Stephanie's dress yet?"

We explained the outcome of the trip the day before, then asked if they knew of any rental places or consignment stores in Brookhaven or McComb. Another one of the girls, Ashley stated, "You don't have to rent a dress. Stephanie and I are about the same size." She turned to Stephanie then and said, "You're welcome to use my dress. I'll bring it tomorrow."

My spirit was humbled. Ashley was both the daughter and the granddaughter of local doctors. Her mother had been Miss Ole Miss. I knew the dress would be gorgeous, befitting the daughter of a King.

It was. The dress was a beautiful blue, a darker hue than Stephanie's eyes. It had a tiny fitted bodice that was heavily beaded. It really was fit for a princess.

I did have a faith-building testimony after all. God did not leave us to find something that would do; He already had in mind the beautiful dress that Stephanie was privileged to wear. He placed a generous spirit in a lovely Christian cheerleader.

SLEEP, BLESSED SLEEP — FEAR NOT: HE IS WITH US!

Dot Day

My paraphrase: *For I don't live to myself alone, and I don't die to myself alone. If I live, I live unto the Lord; if I die, I die into the Lord. So, whether I live or die, I belong to the Lord. Romans 14:7-8.*

Before I became a true believer, I lived in fear. I was anxious in several areas: I had an intense fear of death; my throat closed at the thought of public speaking; I disliked being the center of attention unless I controlled it by drawing attention to myself — I was extremely self-conscious. Nothing I did was quite good enough; I had become a perfectionist in my expectations, far exceeding excellence.

Yes, I was a controlling woman.

All of these areas pointed to my need to control myself and my environment. One can easily imagine the difficulties scarring relationships with my husband and two daughters. I was a nervous sleeper; I was a jealous wife; I lived in fear of making a mistake in the upbringing of our daughters. I was more skilled at manipulation than at being a skilled communicator. I was very concerned with appearance and typically felt a personal inadequacy.

Probably with this self-description, I am harder on myself than most people who knew me would think. I was able to put a mask on and "pretend" to have it together.

One of the worst areas for me was the area of sleep. Major changes had come during our older daughter Sharon's senior year of high school. My husband Charles had been laid off from his job; we had moved from our home in Crystal Springs, a small town of approximately 6,000 people in a predominantly rural area of central Mississippi. We were now living in a house that we were building about seven miles out in the country from the nearest small towns. By building, I don't mean "contracting"; with the help of Charles's family and our friends, we were building a house with full sweat equity.

I slept well the first year of country life. I adjusted pretty quickly to hearing the sound of the birds and other animals without an air conditioner filtering the noise.

Charles had not yet returned to work, and we went to bed together most nights. One night past midnight, I sat in front of the open window of the dining room grading papers. Bleary-eyed and sleepy, I heard what I was later told was probably a male deer. The animal sounded as if were only three feet away on the front porch with only a window screen of protection. I was sure I had heard a black panther!

I jumped up, slammed shut the window, stuck my books and papers in my briefcase, and went to bed so Charles could protect me from whatever animal made that noise.

Soon after that incident, Charles was called back to work. However, he had to work the night shift. My anxieties increased. If the new refrigerator made ice before I went to sleep, I felt compelled to get up for a search and destroy mission. Needless to say, I had in my hand the .22 Ruger pistol with a long barrel.

Sharon warned me that I was going to kill the refrigerator if I shot it. Outside noises produced the same effect; I felt compelled to see what caused the unusual sounds. Again, I might be prowling the grounds of our front four acres of our land in the middle of the night with the gun in my hand. Fortunately or blessedly, I did not shoot our neighbor's cows.

During the next year, at age 42, I became a true believer in Jesus. Much earlier in my life I joined the church and was baptized; I loved Jesus, and I loved his church. I wanted to avoid hell and gain heaven. I thought I was truly a born-again believer.

Over the next thirty years I taught adults in Sunday school, and I taught children in Bible school. I espoused biblical principles through high school English. But I never felt a conviction of myself as an unholy person, a sinner in need of grace. I was faithful in church attendance, a tither, one who visited the unchurched and the elderly: "Doing" all the things a devoted Christian should.

God used the story of Moses's meetings with Pharoah to let me see what I really needed. At first, Pharoah hardened his heart against God's words through Moses. The eventual outcome was that God hardened Pharoah's heart. If I did not submit and surrender, God would harden my heart, truly the unforgivable sin of resisting the Holy Spirit. God was tired of my playing church and wanted all of me, not my works.

On October 12, 1992, I met with our pastor and his wife. Even then, I was resistant. My pride had a stranglehold on me. But I walked out of the office after kneeling and confessing my sin.

I was transformed.

God does not merely change us when we accept Jesus: He transforms us. The word "transform" used in Romans 12:2 is the same word used when Christ was transformed on the Mount of Transfiguration. With God's work we do become new creatures, transforming to the likeness of Christ.

Instead of going outside to seek mooing cows and bugling deer, I prayed for help. God's help came in his Word, Romans 14:7-8. These words provide a supernatural comfort to me in letting me know that my life is in his hands. Because I trust Him, I trust his heart. His every thought of me is one of love. I don't always understand the actions of His hands, but I trust. My response is simply to live for Him.

GRANDMA'S QUILTS
Gail Shows Bouldin

My grandmother, whom we called Mamaw, lived in a time where their only source of heat in the winter was an old fireplace and big heavy quilts to cover soft, fluffy feather beds

To this day, whenever I smell a fireplace on a cold winter morning or wrap myself in one of the many quilts she made in her lifetime, I think of my grandparents.

Grandma had a big quilting frame hanging from her ceiling. When she got ready to make a quilt for her children, grands or other family members, it would be let down. I don't remember the mechanism of how this worked but we were fascinated watching her. Sometimes one of her sisters would be there to help, but as far as I know, this skill or maybe I should say "art" wasn't passed on to either of her daughters or her ten grandchildren. My granddaughter, however, has this wonderful talent.

Growing up, I can remember many times visiting my grandparents. After Grandpa let the fire die down in the fireplace, all the heat we had came from those quilts. It wasn't just one either, more likely three or four.

At that time there was just my little sister and me in our family, and we slept together in a big double bed with a soft feather mattress and piles of quilts. It would be so cold in the room we could see our breath, but we were snug as bugs under Mamaw's quilts. I still remember saying to my little sister, "Let's snuggle up and get warm." Soon Grandma would finish her last-minute chores and come kneel at our bed to pray. Many times we would doze off listening to her praying ... feeling secure, warm, and loved.

Over the years other grandchildren came along, and she would start with the oldest and go to the youngest making us quilts. She never stopped until she had a stroke. Our children came along, and they got quilts, too. Scraps of cloth, old clothes outgrown, our shorts since Grandma didn't approve, and anything else she could find went into a quilt.

Nothing was ever wasted at Grandma's ... Dutch dolls, wedding ring, and so many other designs she made in her quilts, but the most important thing that went into those scraps of cloth, cotton bunting and tiny stitches was love. Grandma has long gone home to her Heavenly Father, but her quilts live on to warm her grands and great grands on cold winter days.

PATTERNS
Gail Shows Bouldin

After we left for Birmingham with my stepfather, things turned abusive between him and my sisters. When my boyfriend, later husband, got out of the Marines, I ran away from home. My sister and I had double dated at the movies the night Terrell and I ran away. I tried to let Gwen know without coming right out and saying it that we were leaving the movies and heading to Mississippi to get married. We were young, stupid and in love, so we just wanted to be together.

Mom had the police meet us in Meridian and put us in jail until they could get there. I was one month away from being eighteen and had dropped out of school. We finally got to Magee and got married. I went to night school and got my General Equivalency Diploma later. Ten years and two children later we divorced. It was a bad marriage, soon followed by another very bad marriage.

I see now that my life was patterned after Mom's in a lot of ways. Anyway, I went to nursing school and was a licensed practical nurse for many years. I was the oldest student in my nursing class, but I didn't care because nursing had always been my dream. I was in the process of looking into getting my prerequisites for a registered nurse associate degree when my second marriage ended and my mother received a lung cancer diagnosis.

I was the only one at the time who was able to care for her and take her to treatments. I worked at night and stayed with her during the day. Gwen and Anne, my sisters, helped when they could. By the time Mom died, I had lost the will to go back to school. I continued to work at our local hospital. Three years later I met my husband through *match.com*.

My life has never been dull. We have been married nearly seventeen years, and I am finally in a good place. All the bad, I learned from. These events only made me a stronger person. We live in Kosciusko where I am hiding out until Covid 19 decides to go away.

"I CHOOSE US"
Dot Day

The impact of the past may affect relationships well into the future. While you may date the adult, you marry the child. Frequently this shows up in arguments and in reaching for solutions.

I am the youngest of eight; my husband is the third of four children. When we look at family dynamics, no one asked our opinions or listened to our dreams and ideas. We became accustomed to being ignored, so we practiced being true introverts. In taking the Myers-Briggs Type Indicator, I found myself to be at the dividing line between introversion and extraversion.

When I was at Copiah-Lincoln Junior College taking an algebra II class to graduate early from high school, I had two roommates. I noted differences between two ways of relating. The time was the mid-to-late 1960s, and we had no talk show hosts telling us how to live our best lives. One of my roommates was painfully shy, almost agoraphobic. The other bounced into others' lives with an introduction of herself and an interest in them. She became quite popular by being sociable and open.

I decided to emulate the second one and found that extraversion suited me. There is still that private, personal individual who can stay silent and closed except to a select few, but there is also the bouncy extraverted person/persona that meets others easily and is genuinely interested in them. Unfortunately, I remain undecided as to which is the natural part of my personality:

Do I wear a mask in socializing to garner others' attention?
Or Did I adopt a role created by my large family who only saw me as the baby mascot of the group?

Our way of relating to others is only one point of difference between my husband and me. But look carefully to see how this plays out through our birth order. Dr. Kevin Leman's birth order book explains this in more detail. But, as people accustomed to being ignored or having our verbal contributions minimized, we had no fighting skills. But we did have a strong need in our relationship to be cherished (me) or respected (him). Reverting to childish ways was not a winning situation.

One thing we brought into marriage was that sometimes you had to get loud to demand what you need or want (him) or you suffer the agony of being silenced by others' angry tones and plot ways to get even (me).

That way of relating spells dysfunction. We became Christians and made some changes, but in arguing, we revert to childhood and compete for our views to be heard and understood. Sometimes.

Other times, we practice the skills of listening, seeking to understand, and ending the competitive battle. He could end the disagreement with an angry "I said so and that is the way it's going to be." I, on the other hand, could win the battle by being quiet, going ahead with my plan — it really is easier to ask forgiveness than to get permission.

In supervision and management courses, there may be an emphasis on win-win situations. How can we both win in a battle? If I win and you win, there is no battle.

Make your adult disagreement a non-battle. The key is to choose the relationship as being more important than either of us as individuals. I have many words and could out-talk him. Thus, I would win. He is the Christian head of the home and could exert his position and role, and he would win. We would be in a superior-inferior relationship with either of these.

If our relationship is to win, one of us must decide "I CHOOSE US." We agree about the big rocks of our relationship foundation — faith, loyalty, intimacy, love, caring, values, support, life goals. However, the little pieces of sand that sift around the big rocks can become irritants if we don't handle them as thinking adults.

When I am active in choosing social engagements or making plans with others, I am also planning how he uses his time. Sometimes I need the reminder that I have planned for him as well as for me.

When I choose us, I defer decisions about planning social engagements or making commitments that require his participation until I have his input. When I respect him (his need), he either accedes to my request or gently reminds me of my limited storehouse of energy and I feel loved (my need).

Oh, and by the way, timing is everything in picking your battles.

At this point, he and I have been married over fifty years and still slip into the battleground instead of being wise to discuss matters. Stressful conditions bring out the worst child in each of us. Our stresses are different, but we both had moments of spoiling.

Remember, I was the youngest of eight and was loved and spoiled by older siblings. Even my brother less than two years older bought candy large enough for us to share. My husband had an injury to his eye and lost his sight in one year. The expectations for him changed as did the demands. Even though each of us had chores, there was spoiling.

Are you spoiled? To recognize a spoiled child, one considers what happens when one does not get his way. Do I throw a temper tantrum or hurl insults? Do I whine and complain? I found passive-aggressive ways of pouting and plotting; he found ways of anger and loudness.

I note that I feel special and cherished when we talk out stress-causing situations. He feels respected when I seek his opinion and value it. Yet, we sometimes revert.

Each age brings new stresses, requiring different adjustments.

I started getting noticeably old when I was around fifty. I could no longer participate in tennis or softball. I could no longer take long walks or climb stairs. I had planned to be one of those fun grandmas who get on the floor and play with her grandchildren, a financially secure woman with no children in school, a wise and respected contributor to society through teaching at least part-time and counseling through a private family therapy practice. I would visit so many new places.

A late-onset muscular dystrophy interfered. I was able to get on the floor when my grandchildren were small, but I needed help rising. I was able to lift each of my granddaughters, but my youngest grandson had to be placed in my arms until he could climb up.

I could not go with them on a mountain hike or play with them at the beach. We were financially secure, but my shopping was online — not at all the same as being in the bookstore. The teaching became too demanding physically and the family counseling was brief sessions to help someone until I could refer onward.

My husband's role changed from partner to care-partner to care-giver. He has managed the adjustment well. Me, not so well.

I am reasonably content and accepting of this unplanned disability. I changed my hobbies and activities regularly to find an outlet and a purpose — drawing and painting, quilting, retreating into books, and now writing.

I drive my power wheelchair as if Indy-bound. I use the Lift Seat to stand me for toileting transfers. I relinquished grocery shopping and trips to Walmart to my husband. I accept that I need help. Most of the time.

Please empathize for a moment. Put a chair beside your bed and sit facing the side you enter. Tie your legs together at calves, knees, thighs, then tie yourself into a leaning-over position. Get into bed without falling. You may be one of those fit individuals who can lever your body into a normal position lying on your back. If you feel you still have control, don't trust your feeling!

You are probably unaware of how many muscles you access or the strength in them. I am fully aware of needing help and yet wanting the independence of doing it myself. However, I need help. He waits beside me for me to ask for it.

However, the fear of falling takes over my nice adult tone when I cannot shift a foot to turn or a knee gives way and I begin my descent to the floor. That part is just the turning. If I am well rested, there are fewer problems.

Once I am seated on the side of the bed, he lifts both legs at once as I push back onto the bed. The next step is body alignment, but you get the idea. My bed positioning is fixed — I sleep only on my back as I cannot turn over. I cannot adjust my covers. We have an adjustable king bed so that some positioning is in my control; however, snuggling and going to sleep intertwined are part of the past. The reverse actions are called for in the morning.

He is a night person; I am a morning person. I might have read the description or heard it or made it up: Opposites attract. In marriages, opposites attack.

He and I are retired. I retired earlier than I wanted because of my disability. He retired early at sixty-two to help care for me. He could sleep late. I am ready to start the day. Unfortunately, he is not. Another difficulty to talk out. Despite the hardship on him, he helps me get up and situated in the chair. Though I would fare better with someone to attend to every need, I don't interrupt his attempt to get more rest.

As in most marriages, we adjust. We also rely on our faith to work toward better acceptance of our differences and even laugh at them and celebrate them. With God's help, we move past "My Way" to His way.

Our decision: We Choose Us, with God's help.

Wayne Dyer noted: Play host to the Holy Spirit or hostage to your ego.

BEYOND BELIEF?

Carl Heard

Over the years, the little country church at Gallman, Mississippi, had its share of ministers in and out, all being of one common denomination, Southern Baptist. As far as I was concerned, that was a good thing.

Brother Jordan appeared on the scene. He was different. I called him our truck-driving preacher because he drove an 18-wheeler for a living. He wore his belt buckle to the side like no other. Now, don't let that title, truck-driving preacher, fool you. His sermons were full of hell, fire, and damnation. He was a true Southern Baptist preacher.

Along with him came his beautiful wife and daughter. As a family they could testify exactly to what our Lord can do. When his wife found out she was expecting their daughter, the doctors told her she had cancer and could not carry the baby. She would have to abort.

Now here comes the part that is so amazing. Because of her stance on abortion, she chose to have the baby. She and her daughter were living proof of our true, living, and loving God.

After many sermons under his truck driving belt, one Sunday Brother Jordan chose a sermon that appeared to be just for me. He used the story of the demon-possessed man, found in Mark 5:1-20 as his text.

Now I had been under attack for over a year. I was depressed; I could not eat; I could not sleep; and I had lost to 98 pounds. I needed to take pills just to get through the day. Despite my having two sons, a toddler and a 12-year-old, there were times I prayed for God to take me home.

After his sermon, Brother Jordan stood for the closing prayer. I stood also and began to pray. It might've been out loud — I'm just not sure. I was filled with the Holy Spirit. Then, all of a sudden, I felt something.

This wonderful power came over me. My praying became stronger, more verbal. Then I felt something warm spewing out of my right ear. I was frightened — beyond scared — but at peace because I knew God was present, and I had been delivered from all oppressions.

The thing I'm ashamed of is it was years before I told anyone what God did for me. I thought people would not believe me. Yet, it is a true story.

THE TIN WHISTLE
Dot Day

Myrtle sighed, putting up her sewing. The children would soon be home from school and hungry. There was more demand on her time than she had time. She had not fixed anything special. She poked holes into two of the flathead biscuits and filled them with butter and sugar. She put them into the oven to warm. Seven or eight hours was a long time for children to wait to eat. They could take biscuits and bacon in syrup cans, but Hank didn't want to look poor. He told Maggie she could wait with him to eat.

"We're hungry, Ma." Maggie repeated these words daily. It took a special day for her to forget being hungry by the time school was out.

She settled them at the makeshift table, pulling the biscuits out for them. She listened to their talk of the day's happenings. Maggie announced, "We pulled names today, and we have to get a present for them."

Myrtle had forgotten to tell first-grader Maggie not to draw names. Hank knew. She looked at him; he shrugged his shoulders and looked away.

Myrtle had hidden the new Sears, Roebuck catalog days earlier. *Why tempt the little ones with toys when there would be no money for a special Christmas?*

"Whose name did you pull?"

"I got Wayne's. He's nice. He and Joel and Hal let me play marbles with them when Charlotte and Laura won't play with me."

If Maggie had only drawn a girl's name, Myrtle could have sewed something for her. Plus, Wayne was probably the most well-off boy of the first grade. His mother was also a widow, but she owned a store.

Hank spoke up. He had tried to assume the role of man of the house after Pa's tractor accident had killed him. "Maggie, you'll have to make Wayne's present. We don't have any money."

Maggie's eyes brimmed with tears. She looked at her mother. "It's true, honey. My sewing doesn't bring in enough money for extras."

Hank was only two years older than Maggie, but a quick and logical thinker. "I can help Maggie. Tomorrow's Saturday. If I can ride the bus to Collins or Prentiss, I'll collect empty coke bottles to turn in for a deposit. And Mr. Astor still owes me for taking care of his hogs when he went to Chicago."

Myrtle stiffened at this news and then relaxed. She cleared the table of crumbs. *How do I say this?*

"Hank, I think getting the deposits is the best idea. I don't think Mr. Astor will pay you though."

"Mama, just because we live on his place doesn't mean he owns us. That was a week of hard work!" Hank's voice rose along with the color in his cheeks.

Myrtle reached onto the upper shelf of the pie safe. The little shotgun house was full of furniture from better days, and she had not gotten rid of any of it. She drew out the catalogue. It had come earlier in the fall. She told Maggie, "You can look at the pictures on the front porch while Hank and I talk."

Maggie's face was bright "Maybe I'll find something for Wayne!"

Mother and son watched her as she clasped the thick paperback catalogue in her arms. Maggie let the screen door slam behind her. She turned and said, "Sorry, I forgot."

Once she was sure Maggie was out of earshot, she turned to her son, "Hank, we live in Mr. Astor's house. He lets us have a garden spot. If you ask him for your money, he might raise our rent or tell us to move."

"Ma, you know he has plenty of money. He went to the Democratic Convention. He gives money in church. He drives a car, sells coffee, and operates three farms. He never did anything to help when Pa died!" The last was the sharpest blow he could deliver, and Hank's voice quivered as he said it. He laid his head, face down, onto his arms folded in front of him on the table.

Myrtle's hand clenched and unclenched repeatedly as she talked with her son. "Son, I didn't want you to take care of his hogs. He had no business getting you to do a man's job. That is dangerous work."

Hank lifted his head. "Ma, he promised to pay me. But the pay he offered was a tin whistle. What do I need with a whistle? Maggie and I needed school shoes."

A cloak of shame engulfed Myrtle, then she became angry at the whole situation. "*Hank was right! I'll see Astor tomorrow. That slimy weasel has taken advantage of us. No more. So what if we have to move? We can move into town, and I'll get paid more for my sewing there.*"

After the three ate a supper of peas, cornbread, and milk, the children sat at the oilcloth-covered table picking out what they would buy if they had money.

Maggie announced, "I'm buying everything on this page. You can't choose any of it."

Hank turned the page and said, "Well, these are all my bicycles, skates, and wagons."

Once again Maggie's eyes threatened tears. Myrtle intervened. "Wash off, then get in the bed. I don't think you'll see these anytime soon."

The next Monday, Myrtle hurried through chores then walked the mile to the Randolph house. Her steps slowed as she approached. Belle and Astor had a beautiful place — flowering shrubs and trees dotted the front lawn. The white frame house had open porches on the front and side. She knocked on the door, peering through sidelights to the hallway. She knew it had a large bedroom on one side and the parlor opposite. Belle's electric wringer washer occupied much of the enclosed porch at the rear of the hallway beyond the second door.

No one responded to her knock. She turned aside to go home. Turning back suddenly she pulled open the door.

Myrtle called out, "Belle? Astor? Anybody home?"

There was still no answer. No odors or cooked bacon or perked coffee. She stepped slowly forward. *What do I think I am doing?* Her heart raced.

She peered into the dark parlor, always immaculate. She continued to call out. Then she turned to leave. A pile of green was sitting on the dresser in the bedroom. Money — more than she'd ever seen.

She looked around, her head swiveling, then picked up two fives from the pile. She thrust them into the pocket of her pinafore. *Astor owes Hank at least $10 for working him without pay.*

She made the trek home in fast time, despite the weight of her guilt. *What on earth did I do? How do I explain this to Hank? Astor owes him. He owes me, too. If he had taught Henry how to operate that tractor safely, he would still be alive.*

Myrtle felt justified and guilty at the same time. *It's up to me now. I have to provide for Hank and Maggie. But I need to teach them about honesty and temptation.*

Myrtle knew what she had to do.

"Lord, help me do the right thing. I can't take matters into my own hands. Henry isn't here to provide for us, but you are. Oh, Jesus, help me make it right."

Myrtle gulped down a glass of water and turned again to walk the mile to the Randolphs.

GRANDPA AND TRIXIE
Gail Shows Bouldin

My Grandpa was, as the old people say, a cut-up in his younger years.

By that, I mean that he was full of fun and laughter, jokes and funny stories especially about his own people. He never outgrew that. He loved to mimic his rather "peculiar," people, as Grandma called them, in ways that would have the listener rolling on the floor. It was not so much the story itself but the way he told it.

Those characters, some long gone, were brought back to life through his retelling over and over. I remember begging him to tell me a certain story that never got old to us kids. He loved to play a lively tune on his fiddle or a sad, plaintive tune that would get his little dog to howling ... which made all of us start laughing. Then Grandpa would say that it was time to stop as it was upsetting Trixie.

Grandpa, or Papaw as we called him, would laugh right along with us, but he loved that dog so much that he didn't want to hurt her ears. He would have Grandma boil chicken to feed to Trixie. The poor dog, covered in a homemade burlap jacket made by Grandma, looked like a big sausage about to burst she was so fat. You would think by her doing this that they were acts of love. Not so! Grandma could barely disguise her distaste at the extravagant love and concern Grandpa bestowed on that little dog.

This behavior was from a man who would never allow a dog in the house, and the dog was lucky if he got to come up on the porch. Grandma was in full agreement with that policy. People back in those days didn't treat dogs as we do today. The men, for the most part, weren't demonstrative in their affection, especially in public, and Papaw was like that. We knew he loved us and would do anything to see that we had what we needed, but I never heard him say "I love you" to anyone ... not even Grandma.

In fact, the one time he did in his older years was such a surprise when Grandma told us how it came about that we marveled about it for years. Anyway, Papaw showered all the love in his heart on Trixie. Nothing was too good for her, and she sat in his lap for hours. My mom and aunt were a little jealous; I think that they had never gotten that kind of attention growing up. Grandma probably was, too.

My aunt used to say that Trixie was demon possessed, but she was just possessive of Papaw. Unconditional love on both sides ... man and dog. One day Trixie got very sick, probably from being so overweight, and she was taken to the vet, an event that would have been unheard of a few years earlier. Everyday Papaw would go to the vet's and stay an hour or so, sometimes more, to comfort Trixie and himself. Trixie stayed in the hospital for several days. I don't remember if she died then or sometime later but when she did, Papaw nearly grieved himself to death.

No one understood that kind of grief except for me, and I didn't fully understand until it happened to me. Papaw lived a long while after Trixie died, but he never got another dog. I think it was after this happened that one Sunday morning at their little country church, waiting for sunrise services to begin outside, that Papaw told Grandma what she meant to him. Maybe his Trixie love and grief opened his heart.

END OF AUGUST
Ashley Chisholm

Throughout the year of 2019, I prayed for a miracle every day. At 26 years old, I was diagnosed with End Stage Renal Disease through a routine doctor's visit. I was told that I was in kidney failure and would need a kidney transplant to live. It was the hardest season of my life, and although my battle with chronic kidney disease will be ongoing for the rest of my life on earth, I have experienced more miracles and blessings than I can count.

There are probably millions of moving pieces God had to line up for me to continue living as I am, so I'll share the short version of events. It all started when my husband RD made me go to the doctor in early spring of 2019. I was hesitant to go because I have always had a phobia of any kind of medical exams and needles. And five years prior to then, I had a major surgery called an Open Myomectomy, so I really had a lot more anxiety than usual surrounding doctor's appointments.

In fact, I was so anxious that I accidentally forgot my purse, license, and insurance card at home. I told RD, "Maybe we ought to just go home and reschedule." This was an office I was visiting for the first time. Thankfully he disagreed and confirmed with the staff that I could still see the doctor. She was very kind and thorough with her check-up exam. When she asked if there was anything in particular we were concerned about, we told her the only thing was that I had been feeling fatigued. She decided to run some additional tests. We had not made it a mile down the road when she called RD and told him to take me straight to the emergency room because my kidney function was at a critical level.

This diagnosis came seemingly out of the blue because kidney disease is called a silent killer; there are few to no symptoms until the disease has progressed into failure. Typically, primary care doctors do not run kidney function tests on younger patients because many insurance companies only pay for older patients to receive a kidney function panel routinely. The only time my kidney function had been tested prior to then was the time when I had my previous surgery in 2014.

Unfortunately, the doctor who performed that surgery misdiagnosed the readings as a UTI instead of kidney disease and never alerted me that my kidney function was around 50 percent. Kidney disease runs in my family. I've had two grandparents, one from each side, who were diagnosed with End Stage Renal Failure in their older age and had to undergo dialysis treatments for several years until they passed.

Whenever someone would ask me what to pray for during that time, I would always say to pray that I can skip dialysis and go straight to the transplant. RD and I, along with the advocacy of my nephrologist to the transplant program coordinators, tried to hasten the scheduling process of extensive testing for both me and any potential donors to get started. But God had other plans for me.

Just a few weeks later, my nephrologist told us that I was at death's door, and it was too dangerous to put off dialysis any longer. Dialysis is a treatment that is a form of life support for kidney failure patients. It takes several hours to complete, or for some, even all night long. It has to be done daily or every other day in order for the patient to live. It can be very restrictive, painful, and harsh on the body. I was on Peritoneal Dialysis which required me to be connected to a large machine every night with a 30+ step sterile connecting process through a series of tubing.

It was one of the most painful things I've experienced, especially in the beginning because I had to start treatments the very next day after having the surgery to place the dialysis access catheter. A one month's supply had to be delivered to me by an eighteen-wheeler, and the boxes were stacked floor to ceiling in our house. For training, RD and I had to attend daily education sessions for about three weeks that lasted the entire day because I was having to undergo actual treatments in the process while learning.

I had a wonderful nurse who we later found out was also my Pawpaw's dialysis nurse when she first started working in that field in the '90s; he had saved her photo in a box of keepsakes we found. Being at the training clinic every day, I had the opportunity to meet and be around other people who were experiencing the same thing as I did. That's when I realized why God hadn't allowed me to skip dialysis and go straight to the transplant. It was in that moment that I knew I had to help my fellow or future dialysis patients, and I couldn't do that if I had not experienced every step and hardship of the process.

When RD and I attended a mandatory group class for the kidney transplant program, the first thing they told us was "You have three options: get a transplant, be on dialysis until you get a transplant, or do nothing and die." It was really hard to share my story and ask anyone for such a large request, but I knew it had to be done. I was completely overwhelmed with gratitude for every person who offered to be tested as a donor candidate.

That portion of the process is protected under HIPAA at the hospital so unless someone told me himself he had signed up, I'd never know. My surgeon told me it was one of the most they've ever had sign up for one person. The testing process is very thorough; they want to make sure the donor is in excellent health before removing his or her spare kidney. With RD being designated as my care partner throughout the surgery and recovery, my parents were evaluated as donor candidates, but neither was able to be approved. The third person to be tested was my father-in-law who lives over 1,000 miles away from where we live in Mississippi but still wanted to donate. He ended up being my God-given match!

When I think about how many different things had to line up perfectly even to be able to meet my soulmate RD and his family, there's no other explanation other than God. It rewinds all the way to my childhood friend who decided to apply to a graduate program in Frostburg, Maryland. Once he moved there, our pastor searched online and recommended a church for him to check out nearby. That church was the one where RD and his family attended. In the summer of 2013, a group of us traveled to visit our friend where I met lots of people from that church, including RD.

About six months later in the new year, I had made plans to travel there again with my friends. But a couple of weeks before we were set to leave, I ended up needing that first surgery in 2014. A lot of people discouraged me from going since I was still in recovery. I tried to get a refund for my airline ticket, but my request was denied. I decided that if I had already paid all that money, I'd rather get an adventure out of it than stay home.

So off I went. It was during that week of traveling that RD and I got to know each other and shortly after started dating. A year later we were married, and not only did I gain an amazing husband, but also an amazing family of in-laws. Little did I know back then that my father-in-law would be my miracle kidney donor!

Fast forward to late spring into summer of 2019. As the weeks went on battling ESRD, my unrelenting and chronic symptoms of debilitating pain, fatigue, nausea, insomnia, weakness, and uremic pruritus rapidly increased each day until they became an unbearable level of intensity, but there was nothing any of my doctors could do.

So, I would pray all day and look forward to the time I would get my new kidney. When the transplant date came around at the end of the summer in 2019, thankfully everything went smoothly for both me and the donor. I was so grateful to be supported by my incredible husband, family, and friends. I don't remember much from that day, but I know it was full of miracles.

Another part of the story that could only be arranged by God was who did our surgeries. My surgeon was a huge blessing because not only was she very skilled at her practice but also extremely kind and encouraging. I don't know how I would have made it through if she weren't there.

My father-in-law's surgeon was also extremely skilled and kind; in addition, they also shared a unique connection. She is originally from Africa, and my in-laws used to live in Africa as medical missionaries (RD's dad is also a surgeon); RD was actually born in Zambia before they moved back to the States. So, between their both being surgeons professionally, Christians, and having a common passion for Africa, it was special.

Another blessing was the timeline. My turn-around time from diagnosis to transplant is extremely uncommon where I live in Mississippi; many people have to wait years to receive a kidney transplant because they aren't able to find a living donor and are forced to wait on a list to receive a viable deceased donor match. And many of those people pass away in the process of waiting. When the dialysis supply delivery driver came back to my house to pick up the dialysis machine after my transplant, he said that was the fastest kidney he'd ever seen.

As immeasurably grateful as I was to be alive with a new kidney, the first week of recovery in the hospital ended up being the hardest week of my life. One thing I was really struggling with was being able to swallow and get used to all of the new medication that I needed to keep my kidney from rejecting. I was probably having to take forty or more pills a day all with new side effects and on an empty stomach because I couldn't eat normally yet. The nausea was indescribable. I did my best to keep down as much medication as I could manage to swallow.

This went on for several weeks even after returning home. Because of this struggle, I was required to be on certain specialized medications a lot longer than most transplant patients. Typically, they taper the recipient down to just the daily anti-rejection medications. Fast-forward to 2020 when the COVID-19 pandemic started. My husband and mother unfortunately caught the virus, and I had been in close contact with them for days. Even though I was extremely immunosuppressed and vulnerable, by a miracle I did not contract the virus. I was still having to take a strong antiviral medication that I was supposed to have been off six months prior. Had I not had all those struggles with the medication in the beginning. I was told by my nephrologist that some of his other patients around my age had passed away after contracting the virus. I really believe God used my weakness and struggle with the medication to orchestrate another step in His plan to save my life.

I've always lived with the mindset that every day is a gift from God, and now more than ever, I know that to be true. Because of my age, I'm likely to need a couple more kidney transplants throughout my life, though I'm still praying for a miracle in technology and medical advancements. God has blessed me with the most supportive and loving family and friends I could ever ask for. And without my husband RD who has taken care of me since the beginning and walked alongside me in the deepest valleys, I don't think I would be here today. Despite all the pain and hardships, I'm thankful God is using our story to be part of His greater plan to help those coming behind me with organ failure and be a witness to his love and provision.

In 2022 I opened an Etsy shop called End of August; the name is in honor of the date when I received my life-saving transplant. I work with partners around the country to design and produce potentially life-saving products at cost. My most ordered item is a t-shirt that reads "Kidney Donor Needed: Ask How You Can Save My Life" on the front and back. My customers are primarily based in America and the UK. I've been so blessed to hear some of their stories about how my designs have helped other people find living kidney donors.

RD and I also own a film and media production company and have been operating it full time together since 2017. Since my transplant, we have been working in collaboration with the two surgeons who helped save my life to develop a documentary surrounding kidney transplants. We pray this will go on to bring awareness and save more lives.

I prayed for one miracle, but I was given many more than that. And God began putting those miracles into place far before I even knew that I needed to pray for one.

"Now to him who is able to do far more abundantly than all that we ask or think, according to the power at work within us, to him be glory in the church and in Christ Jesus throughout all generations, forever and ever."
Ephesians 3:20-21

PLAYING CHURCH

Dot Day

"I was glad when they said unto me, 'Let's go to the house of the Lord.'" ... to play church.

When I was nine or ten years old, I played with Mary Alice and Carolyn. Despite lacking toys and games, we did many things requiring our imagination. One of my favorites was playing church. Their frame house had a side porch screened in to keep the bugs away. Usually there was a stack of clothes in the corner. Maybe their mother came outside to the porch to iron. Maybe they were castoffs. Maybe they were there to be washed eventually. Also on the porch was an old iron bedstead.

That headboard and one or two clothes hangers became a piano in our imagination. One of us played the piano and one of us led the singing. I was usually the preacher; we were in agreement about sin and fornication — we were against it.

None of us knew what it was but it rolled off the tongues of preachers and rolled off of ours just as well. I don't know that we were concerned about sin or our own lost condition No one was transformed by hearing our worship service.

Has our 21st century church also been involved in playing church? We gather together on Sundays, sing praise and worship choruses, adding one or two traditional hymns to satisfy the old people in the congregation. A man stands up to pray impassioned prayers thanking God for his mercy and grace, invoking the Holy Spirit's presence, and then we listen to a preacher pour his heart out. Finally, it's over, and we can go back to our regular routine. Occasionally we do have to give a little money to keep the show going.

Once we have worshipped, we can feel righteous for the week ahead — we are Christians and we proved it. Those who choose not to go to church are at least mentally condemned. So many times our thoughts are not on what they are missing by not being at church, but on mounting our horses of lofty self-righteousness and spirituality.

- We are superior because "my family and I are saved."
- We are superior because we pray for the sick and the lost.
- We are superior because we listen to and understand the preacher's messages.
- We are superior because we hug and greet everybody.
- We are superior as we promise others our prayers for their upcoming challenges.

Well, what's wrong with all of this? The good thing is there's nothing wrong with any of these. We are told to pray for the sick and afflicted among us; we are encouraged to greet others in the name of Jesus; we know we need to listen to the preacher. It is his job to do everything else as a pastor. There are the truly devout scattered among us, those who spend time at home reading the Bible, praying, and ministering. Many of them sacrifice to give money to missions and other ministries.

When the pandemic hit and our lives shut down by federal decree in 2020, the churches had to consider how to do church. It became an accepted practice to use Zoom, Facebook Live, or YouTube to get our weekly message. Nothing was required of us

Ordinary Miracles

except the reminders to send our monies in. We got out of the habit of any type of commitment. This refers to me and my place of worship. I hear you say, "Not me and my church."

Take the following quiz and see how you measure up.

1. I prepare before I go to church.
2. I have a daily quiet time.
3. I seek God's leadership in knowing how and to whom I should minister daily or through the week.
4. I pray before each meal seeking God's blessing, even out in public.
5. I have an area of ministry.
6. I seek to please God, not man.

Back to #1. We check our appearance in the mirror. Clean clothes — check; make-up — check; money for offering — check. Maybe my Bible will match my clothing. If so, I'll carry it. If not, there's a phone app I can use.

Before I go to church, do I pray for the minister, the message, the receptivity of the message? Do I involve myself regularly in Bible study, attending Sunday School where I can speak up, have a question answered or provide answers for others? Or do I pick up my Bible and remove last week's bulletin since I didn't use either during the week?

Do I concern myself more in checking with the family about where we're going to go eat after church? I haven't studied my lesson, but I'm sure I can hold my own with the teacher. After all, I've been going to church all my life. So many my age have fallen away from the church, but I keep going.

See how well I am polishing my crown for my faithfulness!

An area for ministry? Now, what? I am not a teacher — I don't even like to read. Children get on my nerves. Choir takes too much time, and I can't add anything else to my schedule. Committee work is just another opportunity for the leaders to gossip — everything stays the same. I guess that's another thing I'll have time for when I retire.

When I am old, I will have a daily quiet time. That is kind of for folks who don't work. The Lord understands how busy I am with my job, with my family, and all the things I have to do to keep our place together. If my spouse were not so demanding, I would have time.

I'm not really sure what it means to minister to someone, but if I see someone messing up, I'll let them know. I respect their opinions and honor their positions, but some people just need to be told the truth. I pray regularly, just not daily.

We have a limited amount of time when we go out to eat during the workday, and there's no break in the conversation for me to bow my head and pray without causing problems to others. But sometimes we do as a family.

The Bible lets me know there's nothing I can do to lose God's love and nothing I can do to add to his love for me. He is love and he loves me. Surely, he understands my adult need to play church.

After all, I do it for Him.

DISPATCH MEDIC 1! WE NEED YOU 10-8

Josh Dawson

"Dispatch Medic 1, we need you 10-8 priority one to" … These are the first words heard by first responders when sent to help a stranger on the worst day of his life. The words following those 10 "attention getters" can bring fear, trepidation, joy, or aggravation. The next sentence has often contained descriptions of unreal circumstances of pain and terror. The question often posed is, "Are miracles real?" I can testify that He works in mysterious ways, and He provides miracles.

I have been in emergency services for almost two decades and have witnessed many inspirational and tragic situations. What I have come to discover the best question is not if miracles exist but, "How do we perceive miracles?" The Bible talks of the miracles Jesus performed while on earth. These miracles were profound and obvious. The miracles that I have witnessed aren't as easily perceived as a leper's suddenly being healed. The miracles I have noted are as simple as watching a person pass on to the pearly gates with peace and contentment. Those miracles have included travelers who witness someone's losing control of his car and crashing into an area unseen from the roadway. Those miracles are also as profound as seeing a person transitioning from death to life after suffering a massive heart attack.

As a father is watching his son play baseball during a summertime game, he becomes nauseous. He then starts to become dizzy, and his vision is blurry. He walks towards the ambulance posted by the outfield but is able to take only a dozen steps. This father collapses to the hard ground. He has stopped breathing and is lifeless. The EMS crew see this man fall to the ground but aren't rushed into action just yet. Did this man just trip and fall? Was he intoxicated and his feet were bigger than normal? Were we having a medical emergency? As onlookers rush to the man, the medic realizes that this man isn't moving. As the medic leaps from the comfort of his front seat, he's telling his partner "Grab the gear and bring everything." The medic is taking in the scene while moving with purpose to this little spot of dirt.

The father isn't breathing. There's no heartbeat. This is where those years of conditioning switch on and now he's running on reflex. The crowd realizes that "help" is there and heave small sighs of relief. The medic looks into the eyes of another father closest to the tragedy and asks him for help to roll this man onto his back. As chest compressions begin, the medic hears the clanking of the gear he is intimately familiar with being rolled across this hard, dry ground on a stretcher. He turns to his partner and says, "Get on the chest and I will get the gear on."

This man's heart wasn't pumping. By all clinical standards he is dead, in front of these concerned citizens, in front of his wife, in front of his son. As the EMT is pressing this father's chest to the beat of "Staying Alive," the medic is piercing the skin with a way to give a last-ditch effort to give this man a second chance. The lifesaving medicine is going in, as it has so many times before, but the hope is slowly escaping.

These events almost always end the same way: the medic has to look at everyone and confirm their fears. Two breaths, the chest moves with the body's basic needs, and then the miracle. There's a beep, followed by another beep, followed by another. He checks the pulse. There's a pulse!!! The man with the fixed gaze then looks at the medic. The man is rushed to the closest hospital where the staff is in disbelief. Cardiac arrests don't come back, and they surely don't look at you when they come through the emergency room doors.

A few days later, the EMS team is back at that spot. The memory of what happened is still fresh in their hearts and minds. There is a knock on the side, and it's the man's wife. She hands the crew a couple of hamburgers and gives her sincerest "thanks." She then looks at the medic and asks if he has a minute. Well, of course. He always has time to share a conversation with someone he's become so familiar with.

The wife escorts the medic to a man in a wheelchair, and the medic immediately recognizes the eyes. Those are the eyes that were looking at him just a few days ago. This was the man. He stood slowly and was unsteady, but he extended his hand. As the medic extended his, this frail figure pulls him tightly into a strong embrace and thanks him for "bringing him back."

The man returns to his wheelchair and starts recalling what happened. The climax of the story was the man saying that he was in a bright light full of peace and love. He heard a voice. "You aren't finished." The man then looked into the kind, dirty, sweaty face of a stranger, and he knew that he was going to be able to attend another baseball game.

LOVE

Cindy Mount

Love has not come easy for me. Since I was the fifth of six children, it was difficult for me to get much attention. The love in our house was distracted and busy, loud and noisy. My mother did the best she could, but she was only one person in a house of many concerns. Daddy was ever-present for my younger brother and me but always distant emotionally.

The older siblings got much less attention since he worked as a Merchant Marine for twenty-five years and was at sea many months at a time. All of us, except for Tricia, the oldest, were born in Texas. We lived there, moving on multiple occasions, until finally landing in Louisiana when I was five. Mama wanted to go home, and Daddy agreed. At that point, he was a year away from retirement. They built a house a mile from the place where Mama was reared. This would be the only home my brother and I would ever remember.

I was reared Catholic in a predominately Protestant community. That background and living with my father's mental illness and Mama's response to it meant we did not socialize much outside of her siblings and their families who lived nearby.

I've always felt like an outsider, unsure how to navigate life socially. I've been an observer most, if not all, of my life. Very rarely have I ever felt like an active participant in the goings-on around me.

As faithful as my parents were to attend church, we never read the Bible or spoke much about God though there was a Catholic Bible in the house. I can remember feeling sorry my Baptist cousins had to attend Sunday night services because they would miss the Walt Disney and Animal Kingdom shows on television. Those were the days before DVRs or any sort of recording of TV shows.

When puberty hit me, I experienced much depression. My feelings and emotions would wax and wane from highs to lows. It was awful, and I did not handle them well. No one ever modeled for me how to deal with my emotions. Feelings just weren't talked about much, and I never asked that I can recall.

My earliest memory of reading scripture is from my teens. I would lie on my bed reading the Psalms; my heart filled with such longing. I'm sure I must have prayed, but I don't remember. Maybe my heart cries were all that were needed for God to hear me. It wasn't much longer before I met a Protestant girl from a nearby town who decided I was going to be her best friend. She pursued me eagerly, and I loved the attention.

Her father was one of the local doctors. She was the youngest in their family. So, it began that we would spend much time experiencing teenage life together. She had more freedom than I and frequently invited me to spend time with her and her family. Often, I have wondered if the only reason Mama allowed me to spend so much time with her was that her father was a doctor.

Needless to say, this friend and I regularly laughed and cried and did things that only teenagers do. Frequently those decisions were not the best and muddied the waters of my mind. Her freedoms would often create stress for me at home because I wanted to be free in them with her.

There was a lot of confusion in my mind in that season. Once I was able to get out of the house more, I frequently tried to drink the confusion away, many times coming home drunk and suffering the consequences the next day. These decisions did not serve me well. I had no concept of consequences, and I suffered for that.

This friend introduced me to Jesus and kept telling me about grace. I struggled to understand what this meant. In my mind, a person had to work to be approved of to get into heaven. My friend led me to pray the sinner's prayer, and my life changed forever. I wish I could say I became a "good" Christian.

If anything, my life went to hell in a handbasket. I began making bad choices that only made my depression and circumstances worse. At 19, I found myself married and pregnant.

Having my first child gave me a wake-up call in the realization that I was responsible for his little life. So, I attempted to be an adult. Both my husband and I were very immature and self-centered. Our marriage was complicated and messy. Our so very different outlook and priorities created friction that almost broke us.

But God was faithful. He gave me a job with a Christian boss. He put people in my life who exposed His truth to me even if I couldn't seem to grasp it. Slowly, steadily in the midst of stubborn willfulness and ignorance, He planted seeds of eternity in my heart. He protected us from ourselves and those who would harm us.

Somewhere in my mid-twenties, I began attending a women's Bible study on Wednesday nights. We studied a little book called *A Gardener's Look at the Fruits of the Spirit.* The author taught on the parables of the soil from the New Testament. As I read and studied, I became convicted of unbelief. I had always called myself a Christian, but I didn't really know what that involved. The author shared a prayer to ask God to break us of unbelief. I remember earnestly and diligently praying this prayer. The circumstances of my life worsened until I broke.

I finally reached a point in my life where I could no longer pretend that I knew what I was doing or had the answers. This is the time when my husband and I filed for divorce. Now I know not everyone's breaking point is the same, but God knew what it would take to get my attention. He was faithful to hear my prayers. The answers were not quick in being answered. True life change does not happen overnight.

In this season, God woke me up. He began a radical change in my life that I am forever grateful for. So, when I finally reached the end of me at thirty-three and began to believe in God's love for me personally, it was a very big deal.

In that season, God used women who loved Him to manifest His love for me powerfully. His love lit a fire in me that has never gone out. It has flickered a bit in the midst of life's difficult seasons, but God has always been faithful to keep His promises to me.

I'm amazed this sixty-year-old woman can still feel like a child at times, awkward and unsure. God surely created us to be complex people. I have learned a lot over the years. Studying God's word and applying His principles have taken time and effort. I will never regret spending those hours with Him.

These last years the Father has had me looking back. I can see so much more clearly His footprints in my life. He has been infinitely patient with me and ever so gracious. I have been and can be a slow learner and very stubborn in allowing my emotions to rule over me far too many times. Gratefully God is faithful! I can depend on Him instead of those fickle emotions.

> *"The faithful love of the Lord never ends!*
> *His mercies never cease. Great is his faithfulness;*
> *His mercies begin afresh each morning."*
> *Lamentations 3:22-23 (NLT)*

ILLUSION! EPIPHANY! PROCLAMATION!

Janet Taylor-Perry

Illusion — a false idea or conception.
Epiphany — a moment of sudden intuitive understanding; a flash of insight.
Proclamation — a public announcement.

What do you do when not once, but twice, one of your three-year-olds makes a proclamation to shatter other children's illusions after an epiphany regarding Santa Claus?

You laugh; otherwise, you'll cry. It is so NOT funny.

Both my eldest son and my only daughter provided me with two memorable Christmas experiences by such actions.

When my eldest son (I have four.) was three, his father, my now ex-husband, thought believing in Santa Claus would warp the children's perception of God. He took it upon himself to tell our three-year-old son the story of St. Nicholas to explain why we exchange gifts in an attempt to honor a man who gave to the needy. The story of St. Nicholas is heartwarming and real, but not to a three-year-old.

Therefore, when at Mimi and Papaw's house for Christmas, our son proclaimed to his four-year-old cousin, "Santa Claus is dead," childhood illusions shattered. My husband's brother hit the ceiling because he wasn't ready for his daughter to know the truth. In addition, the grandparents were devastated by the turmoil at their Christmas celebration. But wounded feelings healed, and life went on.

By the time my daughter, the third child, was three, my former husband still refused to celebrate Santa Claus, but not so vocally. Although he refused to participate, he turned a blind eye to my attempts to give my children a normal childhood.

My efforts were aided by my aunt and uncle. Uncle Bill was a big man, six-foot-four and three hundred pounds. After he retired, he played Santa in the mall in Laurel, Mississippi, every year. He had no need for padding. My ex often would not go with us to see my family at Christmas. Capitalizing on his absence, I took my four children to the mall to see Santa Claus.

I was expecting number five, and number four was too young to understand. The two older boys understood about Santa, and they knew the man in the mall was Uncle Bill. My daughter was still unsure about the whole situation, but she was afraid to sit on Santa's lap. Her two big brothers sat on his lap, causing her to become brave. The eldest held her hand to go up to Santa. With uncertainty, she climbed onto the man's lap.

With a jolly chuckle as the line for Santa visits and pictures grew, Santa said, "Ho, ho, ho! What do you want for Christmas, little girl?"

Like lightning the epiphany struck! Perhaps the costume deceived my daughter, but not the voice.

With great indignation, she placed her hands on her hips and shrieked so that every child in the mall could hear, "You are not Santa! You're Uncle Bill!"

She jumped down and stalked off, angry at having been tricked. All around, parents grumbled, and children mumbled. My daughter's proclamation of her epiphany regarding Santa shattered childhood illusions.

I wanted to sink into the floor, but by the time we loaded into the car, I was laughing. It was so NOT funny; all I could do was laugh.

Twelve years later, Uncle Bill died a few days before Christmas. Viewing him in his coffin, my son's proclamation came to mind. "Santa Claus is dead." Then, I thought again. Santa Claus could never be dead for Uncle Bill had shown the same Christian charity as St. Nicholas. The spirit of Santa Claus lives even in the hearts of children who had an epiphany and made a proclamation to shatter illusions.

For Bill Ishee, September 25, 1932-December 17, 2007. I love you, Uncle Bill. Your example will always keep Santa Claus alive and well.

FEAR NOT
Averyell A. Kessler

Because of this wretched virus, I didn't go to church Sunday morning.

Instead it came to me. I was up early, sitting in my kitchen with a steaming cup of Community dark roast, when my birds began their usual pre-dawn cacophony of tweets and twitters. Daylight was only minutes away, so I went outside and refilled my birdbaths.

The same group of birds has gathered around my courtyard for years, a band of blue jays, several mourning doves, cardinal families and a mockingbird or two. They form a busy community right outside my patio door. Here, nests are woven and planted in oak branches. Tiny eggs are placed inside, and the waiting begins. I watch and listen as new chicks are hatched, fed, and taught to fly. Most often, my birds are kind, allowing visitors to drop in, bathe and drink, before continuing north for the summer. Sometimes a fight breaks out, when the largest jay challenges an opponent for a spot in the water. It's usually settled after a few minutes of combat, and someone wins.

Last Sunday, a new visitor arrived. As the sky edged to bright, he appeared — a cardinal I'd never seen before swooped down from who knows where. His eyes were bright, like tiny stones in the bottom of a stream. His wings were the color of flame; his head topped with a sassy peak of pointed feathers. He was big enough to take on the big boss blue jay. He perched on the edge of the birdbath, cocked his head and looked around. Safe, all safe. Suddenly he jumped into the water and began his bath. His wings fluttered and whirled, as he tossed off diamond drops. A shiny spray surrounded the birdbath like a sparkling curtain. The next moment, he hopped out of the bath, shook his feathers and sailed over the trees like a rising kite.

So, there he was, a living lesson perfectly in sync with my favorite words in the Bible. "In the beginning God created …." A magnificent creation of God had arrived to remind me of Who is in control and who is not. So, I closed my ears and listened with my heart. Here's what I heard.

> *And shelter you with my wings*
> *As I guard my birds, I also guard you.*
> *Consider the lilies in the field, they do not labor or spin.*
> *Yet Solomon in all his glory was not arrayed like one of these.*
> *If I so clothe the grass in the field which is alive today and tomorrow thrown in an oven*
> *Will I not much more clothe you?*
> *Wake with joy, you are my own. Rejoice in the day, for you are dressed in my garments and walk in my shoes.*
> *As the sun sets, I do not stop watching.*
> *Sleep well, my child, and be not afraid. Evil doesn't even know your name.*

Obviously, these are not all my words, but I remembered and heard them, nonetheless. The lilies quote is from Mathew 6:28. The words "fear not" appear in the Bible over eighty times. Psalm 91 refers to God's wings and feathers. For me, the cardinal was God's emissary.

CHRISTMAS GIFT
Lottie Brent Boggan

"Mercy," he whispered just as the day lightened outside and a sliver of golden daylight slipped through the drawn blinds. The caretaker, Irene, who had lovingly tended to his every need for several months, had been gathering her clothes to go home for the day. When she heard him speak, she dropped them, hurried to his side and slid the bedrail down.

Mercy was the first word he had spoken in almost five days that could be understood. "Mercy," he breathed, on Christmas morning.

This was my beloved husband who has spent almost the last three weeks in Ridgeland Hospice. "My brother Bobby's waiting," he said when ambulance attendants carefully slid him from a gurney onto the bed. He has spoken very little since then.

The time had come when Irene, who had become my dear friend, and I could no longer care for him at home. It was a tough, but a necessary, decision to make to move him to hospice. I must say this: Other than home, I can't imagine another place on God's green earth that would look after my loved one as they have. Although Willard has been treated with respect and tenderness and his every need taken care of, this has been a sad time. Days mixed with hope, then fast falls down steep paths of despair. But we had a few moments to cherish and remember. One was about a week before Christmas on the 19th of December when son Bob, his wife Gail, and grandson Brent drove from Tennessee and came in to see Willard.

"It's my birthday," Bob said to his father.

Willard turned his head. "I know, son."

The four of them had a long, nice visit. Willard was able to talk some. When they were ready to leave, "I love you, Dad," Bob said.

"I love you too, Bob."

Almost since that moment, Willard has been quiet, as if he's now lost in times past. Perhaps, seeing his beloved girls, Pat and Tootie, his granddaughter, Brent, and his brother, Bobby, the young B-29 pilot who was shot down over Yokohama Harbor, years ago.

But, that's not the end of the story.

It was Christmas morning and I arrived shortly after Willard whispered, "Mercy," to Irene.

I sat in a chair by my husband's bed; he was once again fast asleep. This Christmas, known to be the season of joy, has been one of little joy for me and ours. I unwrapped two gifts and set a pair of pictures on a bedside table next to Willard. If he were turned that way and opened his eyes he would see pictures of grandson Bryan Boggan, and the other great-grandson, Carter Ayers. The two have come over and helped me with Willard many times.

The room was quiet. I felt sad and yearned for Christmases past. When I did, the thought came to me: this was almost the end of the Yule season. I had not heard a single carol; there was no Christmas spirit during these long days. I got up, went to the desk at the end of the hall, and told a kind nurse that I felt a real need to hear carols. "I've got a radio here," she said. "There's a station playing twenty-four hours of Christmas music." She brought it into our room, plugged in the radio, and found the station.

I had no idea whether or not Willard could hear, so I turned up the volume and crawled into the hospital bed next to my husband.

As his chin kissed my cheek, I heard the faint roll of drums in the background.

The drums grew stronger.

Willard opened his eyes and looked down at me. Soft voices began singing,

"Come they told me, pa rum pum pum pum
A new born King to see, pa rum pum pum pum.
Our finest gifts we bring, pa rum pum pum pum."

Probably close to the same moment in time, as the voices grew stronger, our son, Bill, his wife, Binnie Jo, their children, Christian and Peyton, were leaving Brandon, coming to see Willard. Maybe for the last time. They would soon be heading out West.

"I played my best for Him, pa rum pum pum pum,"

I gently squeezed my husband's hand. "And oh, you did. You played your best for your King, Your whole life."

Then I began whispering to him, so many of the things I had longed to say but knew he couldn't hear me. But now, oh, he did, and during those precious moments we talked and sweet memories filled the room.

When Bill and his family came into the building, daughter-in-law, Binnie Jo, uttered a prayer, "Please let Willard wake up and know we're here," she asked. "We may never see him again in this life."

He was still awake when they came through the door.

I stood and stepped back.

"How are you, Grand Willard?" Grandson Christian bent over and put his face next to his grandfather's and the two of them spoke quietly. Too soon, my husband grew as still and quiet as a fallen tear.

Dorothy A. Day

Now, there was only an echo of music in the room.

"Then He smiled at me, pa rum pum pum pum."

Since Christmas day our dear one has drifted away again. He may not know we're here, but we can still hold his hand.
And be so grateful for our Christmas gift.

TIPPY TOE DREAMS
Lottie Boggan Brent

A churchy hush filled the Treatment Room as I crawled between soft sheets, and turned on my stomach. A husky, unfamiliar male voice whispered, "Are you okay?" as gentle hands smoothed my hair from my face, coating my neck and shoulders with pungent oils. Trembling, I closed my eyes as strong fingers stole around my ribs.

Soothing, lethargic, oriental music played in the background as flutes made soft whistles and bells tinkled gurgles of pleasure; a blending serenade came from some instrument that could have been a piccolo as it blew out the sounds of rustling wings or unknown creatures sliding through damp, jungly bushes.

I reached across and joined hands with the body on the table next to mine. *I would love for this to go on forever,* I had thought.

Husband Willard and I were on a Caribbean cruise celebrating our anniversary with our two boys and their wives, and they had treated us to a massage.

After the massage, then a gourmet dinner, this unforgotten, treasured day was drawing to a close.

Back in our stateroom, a little too much champagne became my reality and heartburn was my husband's.

Dorothy A. Day

Willard had finished his night by giving me a deep hug, drinking a glass of milk instead of champagne, then dropping off to beddy-bye.

Not quite done yet, raising one more glass of bubbly, I had walked around the small bed and opened the balcony door, watching the shoreline fade from sight. Reflections from Cozumel blinked in sparkling amber colors across the moonlit water as the ship pulled away from the island and headed out to sea.

For some reason, it seemed as if a hand pressed against my chest. I had a hard time breathing. I took deep breaths; I may have felt the window of time slowly closing.

Now, today, January 17, 2021, many years later, on what would have been our sixty-third anniversary, the swinging waves of time roll on.

This night I raise no bubbly, but allow myself a few moments of reflection.

So much time has passed — so many moments slip by, lost in the rising and ebbing tides of time as I write these words. On this special day, as I often do, pages of my memory book were opened and I return to past chapters, reviewing happy moments.

The Boggan family lived across the street from mine, the Brents, on Eagle Avenue. I was just a seven-year-old little girl when I first saw the handsome, dark-haired sailor in his white uniform getting out of a car. So many times after that my friend Ann Hand Dunbar and I used to crouch beneath a magnolia bush or stand tip-toed behind an oak tree and watch for him coming and going, the two of us hiding, pointing and giggling. And I always wanted to see more of him, to talk to him. But, back then, that wasn't to be.

Many years passed before my childhood, toe-standing dreams came true.

I, a divorcee, was working at the hospital admissions desk at University Hospital.

Willard was practicing medicine in Jackson and when he made his evening rounds every afternoon, he and I had developed a speaking acquaintance.

When I heard that Dr. Boggan and his wife were separated I had a heart-stabbing feeling and I thought — *if they don't get back together.*

Late one afternoon, after he had made his University Hospital rounds, Dr. Boggan stopped by my desk.

"When does your husband graduate from medical school?" he asked.

I needed to set the record straight in a hurry. "Oh, we're divorced," I said quickly.

With those words, the good Doctor's attention was flagged. A smile spread across his face, dimples deep enough to grow daisies in showed. "Oh!" He gave a quick hand wave then left.

A short while later the desk phone rang.

"This is Willard and I'd like to ask you something."

"Yes sir," I said.

"Lottie, please don't say sir. I'm recently divorced and called to ask if I could take you to dinner?"

My mouth dry, my heart nearly pounding from my chest, "Oh, yes!" I said.

And from that moment on, oh, those happy years — I thought they'd never end. But, ebbing beneath the tides of time, they did wash away.

Still, death was not the end of our love. I hold you close in my heart.

In the silence of the night I hear your voice, feel the gentle touch of your arm across my shoulders.

And sometimes, when I kinda know I'm misbehaving, I feel those Irish eyes looking down at me. I see a slight head shake, and a deep-dimple grin. "Lottie Bee. Lottie Bee. You know better. Behave yourself, Lottie Bee."

LIVE SENT

Courtney Harris

Leading up to this weekend, I was stressed about many small things and slightly bigger things. I began to question if I am pursuing the right major and truly making the most of my time here in college. I began to be convicted of my posture before the Lord.

I found myself seeking God's blessings but for what purpose?

To answer honestly, it was to make my life easier and more comfortable by just having God "fix it," not to use what God's blessed me with to bless others and bring others to Him.

One of the biggest ways God has blessed me in this season is directing me to this college ministry. First College Ministry has welcomed me with open arms, encouraged me, and challenged me in my walk with Christ. I am so thankful for each person who pours out his time, resources, energy, and heart into this ministry not only to bring others to be saved but to LIVE SENT.

This weekend has challenged me to make the most of my time in college but not through the time I spend studying or getting stuff done, but through walking with Christ and bringing others to know Him. The rest will be important now but irrelevant in the future.

I'm not saying don't study or work hard — actually PLEASE DO. However, ultimately there is only one thing that matters forever, and that is your relationship with Jesus Christ.

Dorothy A. Day

He is Savior and Lord. He can bring you a PEACE and JOY unlike anything else in this world could ever. I have seen this time after time in the little things like before a big test in a class and the big things like when dealing with loss of family or close friends. It does not mean that your life will suddenly become way easier, but having a personal relationship with Jesus allows your perspective to shift and brings you the Holy Spirit to lean on in those hard times. Ultimately, imperfect people cannot bring you peace or joy that lasts beyond a moment. Jesus goes before us to make a place eternally in heaven for those who follow Him and come to know Him as Lord.

"Let not your heart be troubled; you believe in God, believe also in Me. In My Father's house are many mansions; if it were not so, I would have told you. I go to prepare a prepare a place for you." John 14:1-2 @ Twin Lakes Camp and Conference Center

DEAR COURTNEY

Dot Day

August 5, 2022
University of Alabama graduation.

Dear Courtney,

I almost wrote 1922 — a century ago. You would've been dressed in a skirt and a white shirt then. There will be no banking title for you, no heavy thought required. It would be your task just to sit and type and keep the boss's cup full.

You are, instead, young and modern and strong. Wealth advisor. Wealth analyst. Financial whiz. You've chosen to use your knowledge and skill to help others.

Some of my favorite shared memories include you and your sister standing together at the dining room window of the house in Crystal Springs, smiling and waving as we drove up and as we left.

I remember seeing you and Lauren play school and the stacks of problems you created on paper. When Will came along, you continued to school him, and you added the game of restaurant. Y'all made out a menu and took orders; I think the writing part with planning was a favored part. You liked to play dress up and delighted in learning and knowing.

You decided to help me and showed me you were strong. One time the three of us went to Bible school at New Zion Baptist Church, and I stored my walker in the back of the car. It was difficult for me to lift.

"I can do it. Let me." Y'all moved from CS when you were five, so it was little five-year-old you that could and did help.

After the move, your mama always provided good reports. With the teachers, you might have been a little hyper but channeled your energy into helping others; you finished tasks and tests fast and offered your help to those elementary teachers in Sparta.

You have taught me so much over the years, and I miss you. But I thrive on the memories, relationship, and conversation we have shared.

I've delighted in your love for the Lord and pray He will remain your first priority of your life.

I expect great things of you. But I don't expect you to climb high mountains or produce greater art. The greatness of you will be found more simply:

> You will value relationships and people more than things.
> You will feel the presence of Jesus and be led by his Spirit.
> You will adhere to the values of your childhood and youth.
> You will give and demand respect.
> You will not give sway to bullying, either from yourself from others.
> You will speak up for others who are vulnerable and needy, and
> You will seek to help.
> You will acknowledge your own creative spark and let it shine.

My dear granddaughter, Courtney Adele, I love you much. I pray God continues to grace the world with the beauty of your sweet spirit.

Love, Grammy.
PS The check is on its way.

LAYERS OF A PAINTED LIFE

Janet Taylor-Perry

This is my house, my paint, my handiwork. Watching it dry lends a sense of pride and satisfaction. How many layers of change and sorrow does it cover? In time, will it flake away to show old wounds and hurts again? The house stands now shiny and new, brightened by a coat of paint.

The Mediterranean red screams, "Free to be me!" At long last, I feel comfortable enough to make my barn-shaped house look the way I want it to look — damn the neighbors or any critics of my choice. And it looks awesome, neighbors concurring. It has taken sixteen years to get here, but here I stand.

The canary yellow coating on the old house before the red reflected the sunlight with glimmers of hope, the same anticipation for life my soul then felt, but sadly also the same color as my previous home that contained nothing but lies, like the white-washed sepulcher Jesus mentioned in the Bible.

What was this house before — a nauseating faded Pepto Bismol pink? John Cougar Mellencamp's "Little Pink Houses" played through my mind as I scraped the sickening color away. The scraping made my soul raw as if peeling the layers of abuse away could make way for fresh baby skin. The new could not be applied until the old was stripped away. The healing balm slowly dried. My house and I had a new hide.

Before the pink was dull, drab gray, evidence of years of neglect and not being wanted. The wood so ready for any kind of attention soaked even the ugliness of pink into its pores. My life, too, so alone and abandoned, was willing to accept even ugliness to not be ignored. The weathered gray beneath the putrid beige-pink reminds me of the deep bruising on skin and heart. After a while, even the new ugly pink skin flaked away to show the true nature, all the sadness contained beneath.

Surprisingly below the weathered, beaten gray, a few streaks of fresh green remained. The color was one of new life, of spring, of love. I once believed in those things. Like the original color on this old house, those dreams are buried beneath layers of wounds and bandages of paint.

As spots dried on the yellow, it became clear a second coat was needed. Some faint ugliness still shined through. I picked up my brush and began again. One more coat hid the stains and cracked wood and gave the illusion of something bright and happy. One more pep talk, one more counseling session, one more declaration of self-worth was needed to cover the gashes and splinters of my broken spirit.

Stepping away showed the glow once more. Yes, this color was cheerful. Watching it dry to a high sheen let me think. I am so like this old house. It is covered in layers of years, time, and change. I am layer upon layer of life.

The green gave way to love, marriage, a family. The newness was so short-lived. The novelty cracked quickly as the evil gray took root.

How long did that dreariness remain, choking the life from the vessel? Scraping the paint, the gray took the longest to remove. It was stubborn and clung to the old house with a vengeance.

Ordinary Miracles

Eventually the gray gave way to welcome new paint. I, too, broke free, but not without serious damage done to body, mind, and soul. The body heals, but the psyche retains the scars, the stains. I hold no certainty that part will ever heal completely.

The new tender skin was raw. The pink did not handle the ravages of weather well. It had to be reapplied, more than once. Still, some of the old came through, darkening areas. The same is true for my heart. So many areas affected by the strain do not take new paint easily. Shattered dreams, wounded hearts, broken toys, lost trust required many holes to be filled with putty and much scraping to remove roughness.

For a long period, the new skin held. Taking a chance broke the scabs, and the wounds reappeared. Pitted areas on the sides of the wood show hail damage. The old house withstood the challenge. Yet, it begged for something fresh, something new. It can stand alone. Its foundation is firm. The color upon it will reflect the contents.

Yes, sunshine yellow is what I first chose. The color, like daffodils, spoke of a new beginning. I could see the heads of the flowers dance in the reflecting shimmer. I breathed, "Old things are passed away. Behold, all things have become new."

A light touch said the paint was still tacky. I waited a little longer. Not quite cured, the color coat was tender to the touch like certain topics. Some things still hurt to talk about — probably always will. The wounds were deep. It has taken a lot of putty to fill in the cracks and chinks. The wood was the same.

A deep sigh expressed the need to move forward. I can no longer dwell on what was. I looked at the fresh coat and saw what could be. The house stands as assurance. Life goes on. The strong endure. Like this old house, I am strong. I will persevere. I will survive.

It took all day, but the paint dried. The bronze blaze from the setting sun cast a golden gleam onto the new surface. The boards appeared to be filigree. The smell was fresh. None of the sadness showed. I am this old house. This old house is I. As long as it stands, new paint can correct its faults. As long as I stand, my imperfections can be rectified.

The paint was dry, but it felt slick to the touch. For a while, the elements slid off. No rain, no hail, no frost stuck. I am one with this structure. The paint upon my soul was fresh and new. The insults hurled slid away. Nothing hurt me, or so I thought. I had a fresh coating. I, like my home, was shiny and new. I had new skin, a new coat.

I am no longer fresh and green; innocence has evaporated. The bruises have healed. The weathered tarnish is no longer visible. The putrid pink, soft new baby pink, skin has toughened. It was covered in gold. Happiness and contentment reflected in the buttercup yellow. New blooms of jonquils offered latest hope.

The paint was dry. My new skin had grown thick. Still, new becomes old. And more hurts, some deeper than the old piled upon my house and me. The pelting storms required a new roof. A new roof needed a new color. I took a bold leap. I stepped out and followed my dreams, my heart. The house is now red, like its barn shape requires. I am not naïve enough to believe again that the paint will last and not need to be touched up.

It will require maintenance. I will require maintenance. My house will exist one day at a time, as will I. But change will come for both of us. The difference is ... I anticipate change as a challenge to continue to grow. I will continue to exist. Someday, I will be gone. Will this old house still stand? Perhaps. Its foundation is firm, and its inside has been filled with love. Even after I am no more, I can rest assured I have left a legacy of love — It filled my old house.

A DOG MOVES IN

Dot Day

I was hopeless and approaching a situational depression — so many changes occurred at one time. Now unemployed based on my figuring out if I could not lift the textbooks, I probably needed to give up teaching. My family therapy practice had dwindled away when I returned to full-time work for an agency, and I didn't have the stamina to build it again.

Our adult daughters and their young families lived in another state. My closest friends were continuing to work or had already full lives that seemed to have no need to be involved with a woman who could no longer move fast or for very long. The only daily topics of discussion with husband Charles were the latest debates from Fox news or the local stations' news. Even patient husbands tire of politics and murder.

Throughout my work life, I had been more human doing than human being. Active in church, many of my formerly easy activities were closed! If I walked even short distances with a walker, I fell. Trips shopping were fraught with danger — have you ever counted the number of steps to get from the parking lot's designated disabled parking spaces to the store itself?

Well, neither had I, but there were too many for safety. Muscle fatigue caused my knees to give way, and I went down. Gracefully, of course, but down. Plus, I was lonely: I was no longer teaching English to 120 students, and Charles was out of the house at his job. Other job changes and responsibilities had limited my family practice for the preceding seven years. What was I to do?

In came a rescue dog to rescue me! However, let it be known, Lady also saved me from the expense of psychiatric treatment. I had not wanted to retire disabled at the young age of 59 from my teaching career. I had several physical difficulties pushing my decision for a psychiatric referral — mainly I didn't know what to do with myself and was not in good shape from the late-onset muscular dystrophy that invaded my life and severely threatened to take away most of my public identity. Entertaining myself with household cleaning or yard work were no longer options as my need to hold onto a walker increased.

Yes, I needed a psychiatrist. As a family therapist, part of our code of ethics requires that we seek help when we are overwhelmed. I was not handling my life situation with poise and purpose. My neurologist made the referral, and I waited. The psychiatrist's office was slow in calling me for an appointment. With a spark of wisdom and a dash of impulse, I became a dog caretaker. Daughter Sharon had Spud, a Bichon Frise, and I relished the idea of a relationship like theirs.

At that time, we did not have a local animal rescue center. So, I called the nearest one in a town thirty miles away. I explained our situation.

The rescue facility manager described what I needed. "We have a small, sedate, older dog of eight. She has been here most of her life and has enough poodle in her to prevent shedding."

She sounded like the ideal dog. She would move into our house and respond to the love we would lavish on her. She would be an undemanding companion, someone to talk with throughout the day.

We made the trip to visit, not get, a dog on the Saturday before Easter.

Yes, we had a plan. I am sorry to say that dog had no interest in us. We visited her cage, and she was aloof, not the instant friend I had expected. I was as yet un-dog-educated to realize I would need to break her self-protective barriers. How many times had she been left?

I did not at the time believe I was one of those persons who was attracted to the "next bright and shiny object." However, there was a three-month-old puppy who immediately fell in love with me that day — never mind that the person who regularly fed her was behind me as this beguiling tawny pup with the white ruff around her neck threw herself into the wire, standing on hind legs in her attempt to reach me and shower me with love.

Charles had fallen for a hound-looking dog; I think a Catahoula. But I insisted on the pup the rescuers had named Taylor. The grunyons (aka grand young ones) renamed her Lady — well, many other names, but we liked Lady better than Buttercup and Buttermilk.

I succumbed, and all reason and logic flew out the metal doors of the barn-like building. No, we had made no purchases to ready our dog for her unfamiliar change in environment. No, we were just looking, not shopping. No, we or I had lost sight of any wisdom. I ignored the advice of looking at the dog's paws to tell how large the animal would grow to be. Hers were large — but she loved me, and this lonely woman needed the exuberant affection.

I was convinced there would be a queue of people coming in later on this late Saturday evening to claim this particular brown-eyed lass. The only thing to do was to get her today. As I remember it, my husband assured me we could come back after the weekend.

My heart and need for self-indulgent immediate gratification pushed me toward saying, "We'll save money on gas, and we can stop at Walmart to get supplies. Let's take her today." This appealed both to Charles's frugal nature and his willingness to please me.

Her squirming body and energetic yelps as we loaded her into the car should have alerted me: she was more dog than I could handle. I was not paying attention; I was still in the throes of puppy love. We stopped at the local Walmart where un-named by us Taylor soon-to-be Lady eliminated some of the cash in Charles' wallet and enriched him with more space there. Meanwhile, Taylor/Lady had been so rambunctious that she enriched my trousers with some of her not-quite-digested dog chow and my nasal passages with that delectable scent of eau-de-dog puke.

I was still besotted, and those mild inconveniences did not faze me. Soon, we were on to further training of the lass we renamed Lady. I was busy at this new teaching/learning arrangement when I heard the phone ringing. I answered. The voice on the other end stated she was calling to set up my psychiatric visit. I thanked her and explained I had found my purpose.

"Tell the doctor he has been replaced by a puppy."

Her chuckles made my day.

HOW MY DOG SAVED MY SANITY

Or the Benefits of Dog Ownership on Situationally Depressed Me

Dot Day

*I learned to stay in the moment.

Mental health enthusiasts and practitioners place much emphasis on the need for mindfulness and staying in the moment with the anchors of your setting. You know, "You are here in this place. Your feet are firmly on the ground …." Oops, that's a prelude to hypnosis or guided imagery.

With us ruminants of an introspective nature, they encourage not dwelling on the past or anticipating the follies of the future. Guilty of both parts and quite uncertain of my future as a possible invalid, I needed help. And my help was close by. Yes, Lady had moved in, God's answer to too much introspection. Yes, Lady was an answer to prayer.

Without significant therapeutic training, our puppy Lady decided that I needed to focus more on my actual surroundings and relationships. She yipped and yapped (a little louder than a yip) and raced around in her antics and frantic attempts to keep me on a present-moment focus.

If I chose not to be diverted, she created dog-made diversions — she destroyed household goods like clothing or shoes, chewed safe toys to pieces, or moved items like plastic water bottles from the trash to her corner where she broke them down.

To be further demonstrative of her desire or her latent passive aggressiveness, she chewed her Nylabone into the shape of an arrow. Who could resist that threat?

I interacted more with the outdoors.

If I became too involved in a task at my desk or similarly invested in watching the news, Lady interrupted with a head cocked to one side and a little whine. If I changed my attention to her, she smiled and straightened her head while simultaneously tossing it backward to say, "Get up. Let's play outside."

The smart response was to say, "Lady, you want to go for a run?"

Her reaction was an eager run to the door. Once out, I traded my red Rollator walker for an electric scooter. I backed out carefully from the garage, and then we were off to explore the pond, the ditches, the edge of the woods. She delighted in my presence, and I reveled in her enjoyment.

Plus, I liked once again going at an average walking speed. We visited with the neighbor across the street more. If I seemed to like someone, Lady checked the person out as if considering moving domiciles. She barreled to them. If they petted and cooed, she was packing her toys unless I intervened and insisted she stay with us.

I got dressed for the day.

I have a friend who claims to have pantless Thursdays. I believe this to be true. If one is relatively retired, there is no need to dress. Even though I live in a rural area, I cannot yet allow myself to go outside not fully dressed — the meter man might need to check the amount of fuel used — one never knows.

If I were wearing fashionable pajamas and a matching robe, I might consider that as checking off the demands. My sleeping and all-day apparel had become sleep pants and a tank, usually stained with the drop of a bit of food or drink. (Coffee inevitably made its way down the front.)

However, puppies may decide to break for the street or spot a neighbor outside. I didn't like the image of myself trying to look presentable — ahem, decent — chasing a stray, immature canine. Eventually, we were able to establish that two sharp handclaps meant, a "Come immediately back to the porch."

I established a routine.

My routine might have been according to Lady's demands, but there was a certain amount of self-discipline. A pup's need to evacuate inside either means a carpet or rug or training mat. The dog trainer has a choice of cleaning inside (a lengthy, smelly task) or outside. I opted for outside.

Living with us several miles out into rural Copiah County, Mississippi, Lady preferred the great outdoors. She found the edge of the woods allowed her privacy while also giving her opportunity to see me.

My 100 mg. of prednisone on alternate days played with my sleeping and eating habits. Lady and I soon adapted. She awoke me or I awakened her. If I allowed her to be noisy — practicing her wolf howl — she might waken my still-working husband and cause our banishment. We found ourselves enjoying a bit of cheese and sometimes an apple, then went to the great room to play. The final part of our daily night schedule was for unlimited petting of her in my lap as we fell asleep together in the recliner.

**I turned on the lights more often and in more places.*

Rather than sitting in near-darkness "bemoaning my lost estate," I turned on the lights so that Lady had fewer places to hide and tear up the household goods. It was not that I had preferred the dark, but my aforementioned frugal husband had instilled in me the need to have lights on only where I was. But I needed to see at a quick glance that sweet tooth-cutting puppy was using her Nylabone and not my expensive leather shoes.

**I learned to accept the ministry and blessing of others.*

Puppy licks and other non-verbal declarations of love and acceptance encouraged me to allow others to administer caregiving. No longer was I the one tending to the needs of others; I was the recipient. This is a big move for anyone, whether moving into invalidism or not.

We all need to learn to ask for and accept help. If you have someone who seems standoffish in your life, then the best plan is to involve the reluctant one by asking him/her to do something for you. No statistics, but this has been researched; something about your return obligation to them mellows the individual, I suppose.

I gave up inactivity and rumination.

There was no time left in my day for self-pitying thoughts and regrets. When Lady practiced her own quiet time by napping, I resorted to a similar welcome period of distraction-free resting of my eyes.

I had a subject for discussion.

In the past, many people perceived me as needing to be asked how I was doing. That was kind of a conversation killer for me. I could now offer news about Lady's training. She and I frequented the deck waiting for my husband Charles's return from work.

When we heard his Avalanche in the driveway, she learned to respond to my command, "Go see." In time, that came to mean check for company. As she lived with us, she learned many other conversational cues and loved to show them off. Unless she was too excited by the company.

As an addendum, I sometimes offer relationship help to others who seek me out and come to our home. Lady is large for an indoor dog and sheds profusely, but she is one of the most therapeutic tools in my arsenal. She immediately garners attention and is welcoming of others' attention, thereby putting others at ease.

Instant rapport!

THERAPY LADY

Dot Day

The client entered my home, no, Lady's home. Our rescue mix dog was the official greeter and hostess whenever someone appeared either as a guest or as a counselee.

Brenda spoke to Lady and then sank down into an armchair. When she was seated, Lady's greeting job is considered over, and she lay on her blanket to hear Brenda's story.

As she told her story, Brenda sobbed because she thought she had messed up her life. I pushed the box of tissues closer to her; Brenda did not take the cue immediately, so I removed an individual tissue myself.

Lady sat up, cocked her head, and pointed her ears upward. She stood, poised to act. Lady was now five years old; she had been with us since she was five months old when we chose her at the nearest rescue center.

Within that immediate past year, I had given up my teaching career, allowed my counseling practice to dwindle to almost no clients, and gone from almost daily interaction with people to seeing only my husband Charles who was continuing to work. A late-onset muscular dystrophy had changed pretty much my whole life.

The 61-year-old me didn't like the pity party I was hosting for myself and asked my doctor for a referral to a psychiatrist.

He agreed to have a psychiatrist set me up with an appointment. However, the promised appointment was slow in being scheduled.

In the intervening time of waiting for his call, I decided I needed a dog. A dog would be a companion, would give me purpose, and might be fun to train. An older, mature, sociable dog with no awkward behaviors and needing a forever home was my goal.

I convinced Charles and then called the shelter. The director told me they had one that matched my description perfectly.

The smiling director opened the door leading to the kennels, large cages for each dog. An almost golden puppy with a large white ruff around its neck with the small pointed ears of a shepherd stood on her hind legs in her eagerness to greet us.

There was no need to look further — we had found our dog.

Indeed within a week she had provided what I needed: a sense of purpose and a willing student.

Brenda continued to sob. I was not close enough to hand her an individual tissue. My attempt to stand might interrupt her gush of tears and extinguish her flow of words.

Lady determined to take charge. She came to me taking the tissue from my hand. Both Brenda and I watched in surprise as she headed toward Brenda. *Surely she's not going to give the tissue to Brenda.*

Lady bypassed Brenda to return to her bed. Then the laughter came for a moment; Brenda selected a tissue and resumed her story before returning to her tears. Evidently Lady tired of her own boring tissue with no interesting human secretions. She left behind her own now-shredded tissue, sidled up to the armchair and put her head on Brenda's knee.

Brenda interrupted her misery to respond to Lady; after a couple of pats and behind the ear rubs, Lady grabbed Brenda's tear-soaked tissue and returned to her pillow.

Brenda left her tears at an end as we worked on solutions for her problem.

STOMACH STAPLES AND A CYCLONE!

Janet Taylor-Perry

I've had five C-sections! Yeah, yeah. I see your mouths agape. You're thinking, no way! Yes, way, but that is not the funny story here. Oh, no, that is only the set-up. The story itself is so NOT funny, you have to laugh.

My youngest child was delivered by C-section on April 12, 1996. No problems — a healthy baby boy who weighed in at eight pounds and six ounces, 21½ inches long. Now, everybody knows how insurance companies hate to pay for hospital stays. So, baby and momma were cut loose two days later, April 14th. Happy birthday to me!

Yep! I got to take my son home on my birthday. I was so hoping for my husband to stop and get me an ice cream cake. No go.

Sloshing rain pelted the covered area of the hospital where we loaded into our little Sentra, baby in back in the proper child seat and me up front. Needless to say, the seatbelt wasn't comfortable across my incision closed with staples. Now, if you don't know about staples in the abdomen, it makes it darn near impossible to stand straight. Still, home we went. I'm glad we had a carport that kept us from being drenched.

Under normal circumstances, church ladies would've had lunch waiting for us upon arrival, but the weather was horrendous and it was Sunday, which resulted in the husband unloading baby and me and going back out in the pounding precipitation to grab us a bite to eat.

I lowered myself onto the couch with the baby beside me. The husband had handed me the cordless phone in case I needed anything before he returned. I was set.

My brother-in-law was notorious for forgetting my birthday was the 14th and usually called me on Tax Day. Not this time! He got it right. The phone rang, and I received my birthday greeting from Connecticut. We talked, and he said he'd keep me company on the phone until his brother returned. Baby Samuel Taylor Perry slept soundly, so this was pleasant.

Five minutes into the conversation, our tornado alarms went off. Living in Mississippi, one does not ignore the tornado alerts! One takes cover.

I got off the phone, hobbled to the enclosed bathroom, laid the baby in the bathtub, rounded up my two cats, and P.C. (You can read about the characters they spawned in *King Satin's Realm*.) I put them under the cabinet beneath the lavatory, and went to the back door to wrangle Lightning, my 80-pound half German shepherd and half Chow dog, who thought he was a lap dog, into the bathroom. The dog instantly jumped into the tub and lay beside the baby in protective overdrive. There was no way I could sit in the "safe" position, kneeling against the wall with my head and neck covered. It was all I could manage to sit on the toilet seat I let down.

To make matters worse, the power went off! For a good half hour, I sat in total darkness, listening to little tongue laps against the baby who seemed content, hissing and yowling cats locked together in a cabinet, howling winds, and hail pelting my roof. No husband came in — he was stranded at the Wendy's for the duration of the storm.

After a seeming eternity, the bathroom door opened. Still no electricity, but there was food, and the alarms had stopped. The husband lifted the Wendy's bags with a grin. "At least we'll have an interesting story to tell Sam about his homecoming."

Sam is all grown up, one fine specimen of a young man. I guess I need to get a big stick to beat off the girls — Oops! Too late, he's married. Looking back, it really is funny. At the time, having stomach staples during a cyclone was so NOT funny, and laughing made it hurt even more!

TELE-PHONY

Dot Ainsworth Day

Wilma hummed as she put the last pot in the drainer. A smile played about her lips as she walked into the dining room, ran her fingers over the sleek oak cabinet, and then picked up the earpiece.

"Miss Vera, get me number 723, Leona Ainsworth."

Wilma, a solid-figured woman with bird legs smoothed her over-processed frizzy black hair away from her face, straightened her spine and squared her shoulders. "Hello, Leona, is that you? You sound different …."

"Guess what? … Yes, I have a phone now, but that's not my big news. Clifton got put on with the court as a bailiff. He'll also get to work forty hours each weekend as the jailer."

She listened for a minute and then responded, "Uh huh. Well, I get to make meals for the jail." She paused, listening, her mouth pursed.

Wilma sniffed. "Hmph, new job, nothing I haven't been doing for at least twenty-five years. It can't be any harder than fixing meals during cotton-picking season. I've got to make three meals a day anyway."

She cocked her head to the side as she listened. "It's gonna be so nice with a little extra money." ….

"How hard can it be?"

After a brief pause, Wilma continued, "The jail only holds fifteen people, plus any workers on the shift. Usually there's not that many in there. The only big day will be Sunday if people cut loose on Saturday nights."

The two sisters exchanged pleasantries about everyday life and were about to make their goodbyes.

Wilma said, "You must be on a party line; somebody's picking up the phone and then banging it down. There's only one other person on the line with us ...."

"Eight? Ridiculous. That is entirely too many families on one line. It is just a shame that y'all can't move to town and find work. How do you ever get to call anybody? Don't bother to answer. That rude person must need to use the line for an emergency. We'll talk later ... Bye."

She needed to get to work. First, plan sample menus for the sheriff to make his pick. Second, figure exact prices for the items she had on the menu. It all had to fit the budgeted amount.

Wilma worked for an hour, and the phone rang. She made her way to the telephone corner and answered.

"Oh, Clifton, I am so glad it's you. Finally, I won over on Leona. She might've gotten her phone first, but I have one now. I could tell she is jealous because we live in town and have jobs."

After listening for a minute, Wilma said. "Nine tonight for supper? I didn't think my job had started yet." She listened with her eyes darting around the room. "Okay. I can do that, but the meal will be real simple."

She ended the call, picked up her paperwork, and stacked it. She picked up the olive-green ledger, made notes, and dated the entry. Grabbing her purse, she headed out the door. Before she could leave, the phone made its insistent tinny demand.

"Yes, this is the lady of the house ...." She confirmed her phone number and address. "He installed it this morning .... The worker had perfect manners; he was very respectful. He even took his shoes off not to track my floors ... I already used it and understand it. I didn't need any instructions ... What cleanup and blow out? Now, Miz Brown, I never heard of such a thing; what do I need to do? Hold on while I get my pencil."

She got her paper and pencil and came back to the phone. "First, I need to cover everything?

Just the things I don't want dust on." Wilma's brow scrunched up as she looked around. "How long do I have to be away from the house? ... Well, I have a job. I'll have to work with my schedule."

She pushed her glasses farther back on her nose. "Is there anything else I need to do? Will someone come here from the telephone company?" She groped for the nearly out-of-reach clipboard by extending the earpiece cord as far as it would go. She grabbed the clipboard and turned a few pages to find an empty one.

"One of them is in a large pot. Can I just cover it? Okay, we can do that; it's going to be a lot of extra work what with washing all the sheets and towels and me with a brand-new job." She paused, looking around the room. "It might as well be this afternoon."

After listening and jotting some notes, Wilma hung up the telephone. She mumbled to herself. *Let me redo my list to be sure I've got everything. I need to put up our food items, cover anything that might get dusty in the room with the telephone and in the rooms on either side. If the telephone rings, I'm not supposed to answer it. A call at 2:00 will announce the start. We can't be in the house for an hour. How in the world will I get it all done and cook and wash clothes?*

Back to the phone she went. "Leona, have you ever heard of a telephone blowout to clean up the lines?" She listened.

"I don't see how just two people on a line differs from having eight people. You ought to have to clean up your lines if I hafta clean up mine ... Well, I've got to go, I'm cooking tonight and each meal tomorrow."

Wilma hung up the phone and got busy. She and her son wrestled the large green schefflera into the little wagon to take to the side porch while the two girls brought out all the extra sheets and towels. "Let's bring out the dining chairs and footstools, so we won't use all the sheets to cover them."

Soon the three had the furniture covered or moved, and the house closed up tight.

"This will be such a mess. Dirt, grime, washing clothes and jail meals. It'll take up to midnight to get done. I hope the inmates will eat corn bread and milk for supper. But that can't be the first meal I fix." She was ready to cry in frustration.

Done with the chores and ready for the clean-out of the phone line, Wilma and her three pre-teen children settled themselves on the side porch. The phone made its tinny summons. Anne offered to answer it.

"No, we can't answer the phone for the next hour. Probably that's the call letting us know they're starting the blowout."

CJ cupped his fingers around his eyes, shielding them from glare as he pressed close to the window. "I don't see anything happening, but I can't see very well."

The phone persisted ringing until they had seven calls within a one-hour space, each with eight or nine rings.

The quartet moved back inside; nothing had changed. Wilma was speechless. The phone rang again, and she snatched it up. She listened briefly.

"Listen to me, Miss Ida Mae Brown. I'm not doing this for fun. It's too much trouble. Reschedule nothing. You can't ...."

"Leona, I ought to spank you. Shame on you, little sister. You know how busy I've been. Shame on you for pulling this trick. Shame. Shame. You might have won this round, but I'm coming for you."

HAGAR
Janet W. Ferguson

Genesis 16, Genesis 21, Galatians 4:22-31

Honestly, I never liked Hagar.
But then I never put myself in her sandals.

She was a slave. She never had any choice about how her life would go. Although, sometimes we feel like we have no choice, I don't think in the modern United States we can quite imagine her predicament fully.

She was an Egyptian. She may have been given to Sarah by the king of Egypt when he asked them to leave after the debacle of taking Sarah into his harem. Then she was given to become Abraham's secondary wife when Sarah could not conceive.

I don't want to imagine that! But Hagar obeyed her master.

Once Sarah had taken matters of providing an heir into her own hands (instead of God's) and insisted Abraham take Hagar as a wife and Hagar conceived, the servant Hagar despised her mistress Sarah.

Note, Abraham like Adam went along with his wife's plan. It's interesting how much influence wives can wield over their husbands.

How did Hagar act when it says she despised Sarah? Perhaps proudly with boasts or insultingly with cruel remarks to Sarah. Or maybe with just snide looks and ugly smirks. As women, we've seen or possibly given those. Somehow though, Hagar thinks herself in a higher position now than Sarah, and she lets Sarah know it.

And pride goes before Hagar's fall.

Sarah complained to Abraham, and he left Hagar out to dry, telling Sarah to do whatever she thought best. So Hagar had been wrong in her assumptions of her place, no matter her intimacy with Abraham. That probably hurt.

Sarah mistreated Hagar so badly (I'm not sure how, beatings, maybe?) that she ran away into the dry wilderness. Perhaps back toward Egypt. Alone and pregnant, she must have been pretty desperate to do so. She doesn't seem to stop until she's out of water, probably weary and parched. Hopeless. Pregnancy and desert running are not a good mix.

Then God shows up.

Maybe I shouldn't have been so quick to dislike Hagar. Because I've committed the sin of pride. And in the past, I've found myself running until I can run no more. I was at the end of my own strength. Then I finally listened for God's truth. Sadly, because I had nowhere else to turn.

So God sent an angel to Hagar. He tells her to go back and serve her mistress and submit. Interesting — God sends a messenger for an Egyptian servant. He still cares for her, no matter her race or background.

And Hagar obeyed God.

Occasionally, God may have to send some sort of messenger to remind me to submit when I become prideful. Whether it's a friend or a health problem or a sermon. Ever happen to you?

Hagar makes this testimony. "You are the God who sees me."

He sees us too. And I'm so blessed by that.

NEXT BREATH, HEAVEN
Dot Day

I collect. Or, maybe I accumulate. Not the passionate researcher who considers provenance, value, I accumulate whimsical curiosities: music boxes, tea pots, blue items, bird houses, and books, of course. These are scattered in with a myriad of "grunions'" photographs — pictures of Madalyn, Courtney, Lauren, and Will.

Bits of writing, both mine and others, are in my paper collection, certain to become articles for *Ordinary Miracles* or *Battles: Glimpses of Truth*. There are stacks of paper to become two novels, one of stories from years ago, files to help me publish, get an agent, or to market.

Yet, the unusual papers are obituaries.

My advancing years and reflective nature help me concur with words of John Donne:

Any man's death diminishes me because I am involved in mankind. And, therefore, never send to know for whom the bell tolls; it tolls for thee.

Heather Linde has written several books tying together the essay-obituaries she penned for her local paper in Alaska. These character portraits became so well-respected she was asked to be a featured speaker at funerals because of the down-to-earth verbal pictures. Several books resulted from these.

One of the first obituaries I collected was written by a loving wife and colleague Nancy Belknap, for her deceased husband, the professional man who fathered two sons of strong character and reputation. I had seen Nancy and her husband at several school functions over the years, but I failed in getting to know the man who danced her beautifully around the room. I had seen the two dance, but I knew nothing of him. The obituary was personal and differently written from the factual one. John Wayne Belknap was a basket weaver, using strips of wood from trees he chose himself. His professional achievements were mentioned, but I have remembered the detail of basket weaving. This personal glance told me more than the list of professional achievements and the roles in which he served. Nancy stated she wanted their grandchildren to know of his love for the natural world.

A former student and recent widow, Linda Guynes Channell, allowed me the use of her husband's obituary.

"Ronnie Channell was born on December 15, 1951, in Hazlehurst, MS, and humbly entered through the gates of heaven on February 24, 2023, after spending a really good and peaceful day on the land he loved with people he loved more.

"Ronnie was a man who was the epitome of community. He was most at peace when he was surrounded by the people he loved in the places he loved. Whether he was sitting in the Masonic Lodge and telling old stories about family and growing up in the Dentville community, or growing vegetables and spending time on the land around Crystal Springs with his beloved children and grandchildren, Ronnie always took the time to notice his neighbors and look for ways to serve others. He invested in the lives of so many around him, putting others ahead of himself and serving as a role model for countless young men over the years.

Ordinary Miracles

"Ronnie spent enough time in and out of doctor's offices and hospitals to know that all time spent with those he loved was a treasure not to be taken for granted or wasted. He was a giver in the truest sense of the word, content in supporting those around him by working behind the scenes and doing his best to stay out of the spotlight. Ronnie understood the importance of community and family and lived in such a way that he will be remembered as one of those truly good guys.

"Ronnie loved to grow things, and that began with his family. He built a life with Linda, his wife of just shy of 50 years. Theirs is a story of mutual love and support, and even after half a century together, his eyes still lit up whenever she entered the room. When Linda's career adventures took her all over the world, Ronnie was her biggest cheerleader. He was content holding down the fort, patiently awaiting her return and ready to hear her stories of elephant rides and the foreign dignitaries she had met along the way.

"Together they created Jennifer McGrew (Keith) and Truett (Kristle), who continued to bless his life by adding three grandchildren, Gracie, Clay, and Jake Channell, to his family tree. Alongside those branches include siblings, Robert Earl, Jimmy, and Susan Channell Hill and a host of extended family and friends. Like countless others in Ronnie's life, they will spend the rest of their lives reaping the rewards of the love he invested in them.

"Ronnie was a good man, full of sacrifice and integrity. The best way to honor him is to love like he did. Tell stories about him, and be sure to make some of your own. Notice the details and act in kindness. Grow some squash or tomatoes, and give most of it away. Send flowers to those you love — just because."

Reverend Frank Pollard of the First Baptist Church, Jackson, Mississippi, was the subject of another obituary. I'm sure many words were spoken as he was eulogized — this gifted man of God. He and I shared an elevator coming from the church's parking lot to get us to the second level crosswalk over busy North State

Street. There was a palpable presence of God present in our brief exchange of greetings. Some men and women are so spirit-led and spirit-filled that one can feel it.

Two others with a strong sense of the presence of God leaking onto others were Joel and Mary Haire — the spiritual leaders at First Baptist Church, Crystal Springs, Mississippi, and probably best filling the role of the townspeople's ministerial couple. As a couple, we saw them at various town and church events though Charles and I didn't attend the church he pastored. I admired the landscaping of their two homes, carefully tended by the couple. Mary had an artistic eye for detail, and the two shared the tasks, faithfully maintaining the appearance. Appropriately, the two died within a short time of each other. It was noted "he was known for his kindness, humble spirit, and consistent lifestyle." He was another whose spirit testified of his spending time with the Master. It seems impossible to think of Brother Haire without also thinking of his wife Mary. She was the epitome of pastors' wives. Brother Haire's ministry partner, Mary was also a leader and role model in the church. Townspeople and passersby saw her as a gifted landscape artist. Those who visited in her home admired her acumen and talent in decorating their Victorian home with antiques. She had an eye for meticulous detail, but mostly she was a woman with Heaven in her heart, who relished the simple joys of Christian womanhood.

James Beasley basically was our town's song leader. Well, not really. But it seems that way. He and I have in common attendance and matriculation from Mississippi College where he was a long-distance runner. I didn't know him there, but I remembered seeing him and others running out in the country. Of James W. Beasley it was said he "left this earth and stepped through the door of eternity ... God used his life to write beautiful stories in the lives of hundreds if not thousands of people." His funeral was streamed online, and I heard of his passing, surrounded by family members who sang, quoted scripture, and shared memories. In the memorial section of the local funeral parlor, someone noted James Beasley "was absolutely the most joyful person; he loved Jesus, and he loved people." A former youth that James had known commented, "The way [he] lived [his] life is a testament to [his] devotion to the kingdom ... My life is better for His love that shone through [James Beasley]."

Covid took others making too many obituaries. For a long time — a two-year period, I kept a list of these I had known, admired, cared for. The length of the list grew depressingly long, and I stopped adding names to it. I don't have regular contact with many people, so I can play with a denial of my feelings and remind myself of the lovely words I had read that were spoken about them.

My former student, Susan Knight still lives. She has in recent years experienced breast cancer surgery and treatment, spots on pancreas and lung with major surgery. While she was recovering from one of her procedures, she fell and broke her hip. Despite her "circumstances," her faith and hope have remained strong. She manages the family's barbeque restaurant in our small town. Charles goes every couple of weeks to pick up plate lunches for us. One day, I rode in with him, but remained in the car. He told Susan that I was outside when she asked about me. She followed him back to the car to visit. We talked briefly about mutual acquaintances and shared prayer concerns.

I told her of my fear of dying. I'm not afraid of death; I'm not afraid of the destination on the other side. I do fear the spector of death in the sense of shallow breathing or pain and suffering. But, her words were encouraging: "What's there to fear? Our last breath on Earth, then the next one, Heaven." She carries Heaven in her heart as do I. Most of the ones whose obituaries I collected have this same claim. But what does death mean for a Christian? Nothing. We do not die. Jesus made the way and provides eternal life for us.

I think of TK. He was on the ventilator for several months being treated for Covid. His wife Dawn knew he was a Christian, but to her he was not as devoted and in love with Jesus as she was.

As often as possible a family member sat with him. His father, Tommy, though not in the best of health, drove daily to Jackson from Crystal Springs to return home in the evening to rest for the next day's return journey.

Dawn told in a Facebook posting of the attempt to wean her husband off the ventilator. When the tubing was removed and he could talk again, he repeated a refrain: "I love Jesus!" There was no doubt Whose presence became real to him while he was locked away from everyone on the ventilator.

There are several biblical passages that let us have hope regarding this passing.

Luke 9:28-36

What do we do with a mountaintop experience? These verses show Jesus with Elijah and Moses, Old Testament heroes whose lifetimes were centuries earlier. For the three on-lookers, disciples James, Peter, and John, it was a supernatural miracle of time and place. The three recognized the two prophets of old. This one little fact tucked away in the account of a miracle lets us know that in Heaven we will recognize others. *We will know and be known.*

Like many of us, instead of resting in the miracle, the disciples wanted to do something. "Let us put up three shelters — one for you, one for Moses, and one for Elijah."

Peter's words were swallowed up by a voice coming from a dark cloud that surrounded them, "This is my Son, whom I have chosen; listen to him."

Thoughts of building tabernacles dwindled away with God's words. The three resumed their work with Jesus. Muscular, stubborn, strong-willed Peter continued to learn to follow Jesus' will rather than his own.

But, when it comes to Heaven, remember: You will know and be known.

Next breath, Heaven! Sounds good, doesn't it?

THE MUSINGS OF PAULINE

Pauline Rule

INTRODUCTION
Miracles of New Life — Pauline Rule

Today, I was given the rare privilege of experiencing new life. Our next-door neighbor's cat was having kittens. I didn't watch the yucky part, but I did see the new-born baby kitten. The proud mother was licking her and meowing as if to say, "Look at my baby! Look at this new life. Look at the miracle and splendor and joy this little life can give. It's helpless now, but one day it will grow and give back life."

You may not be a cat person. I'm not either, but the story has such strong meaning for us I had to share it, and I must admit it was a really awesome birthday party. I can only imagine God at the first birthday party. I see him kinda like this little mother cat, holding Adam's newly formed body up to His lips to breathe life into Him and then saying, "You are weak now, but you will grow and give back the life that I have given you."

Anything I could have said about this mother and her kitten would have paled in comparison to the look on the mother cat's face. In a language that needs no words, I can imagine that the look on God's face said, "I am the giver of life." I see Him at that time becoming emotionally, physically, and spiritually attached to Adam. He made a commitment to Adam to love him, raise him and guide him. Adam was His son just like you are. God is committed to our growth and development and to getting us home with Him so He can hold us for eternity

The master deceiver came along. I am not talking about Eve; I am talking about Satan. He came between God and Adam because he wanted to destroy their relationship. He did cause them lots of grief, but our Father will always take us back and love us. We are His number one concern. I am not saying that before God came to talk to Adam after he had sinned that God did not have to sit down in a cool place and remember that time He gave birth to Adam and reflect on the intimacy of their relationship. God was hurt. We would have been too.

He was hurt but not willing to give up on the relationship. We can all learn something valuable from this. Staying power. So, you have been hurt; God understands. So, somebody did something they told you they wouldn't: God understands. So, you were betrayed, and they chose someone else over you; God understands. God realized at that point the fight for His child would take His own life. He got up and headed to the garden.

Truth is, He could not give up on Adam; he was God's son. Jesus came and died. In a language no words could describe He breathed new life into His children. He wanted to die in your place because you are everything to Him. He may have to discipline you or let you take responsibility for your actions and face the consequences, but like every good parent He will be there right with you suffering through it with you.

Sometimes we have an image of our parents the way we want them to be and don't really see them for who they are. I mean I see my mom as my mom. There to serve me and I sorta take her for granted. Others in the workplace see her as a vital part to their success. They see her as a brilliant businesswoman. I know she is successful, but she is just my mom. You get it. Sometimes we miss the potential of those around us and never fully recognize who they are.

I say this to say we may have a picture of Jesus. We may not see Him as He really is; we may just see the image we have created in our minds. That limits His ability to work in our lives.

While on earth Jesus told us about Himself. He gave us an autobiographic view of Himself.

"I AM COME"

It is Monday, September 25, 2000, in Sydney, Australia. "All the eyes of Australia are on what has been written as "Our Race" run by "Our Cathy." Cathy Freeman is a young Aboriginal girl who really is not much different than most girls her age. The one thing that causes her to steal the heart of all Australia is her ability to run. In her own words she declares, "This is my moment to be a symbol to my people."

She lights the Olympic caldron, and all the weight of Australia now rides on her shoulders as the 400m race is set to begin. She has burned out her life training for this moment. An American woman is sitting in my living room watching and hoping Cathy Freeman will win this race. 110,000 people in stadium Australia, 5,000 or more outside the stadium. 7,000 in downtown Sydney, and millions around the world are focused on the race. Pressure builds as the gun sounds. In 50 seconds Cathy Freeman experiences her defining moment. She falls to the track as tears stream from her eyes. She grabs the Aboriginal Flag and the Australian flag and makes a victory lap for the people, all the people of Australia.

A Victory for the common man, for someone who had in early years felt inferior to another race of people. She stands on the victory podium with a smile on her face as 110,000 and one Australians sing "The National Anthem of Australia." She has done it and done it well.

George Bush, Jr. sits in a chair having an informal conversation with Oprah Winfrey. She asks him to name one thing he is sure of. He answers, "There is a God."

She nods her head and says to him, "What was your defining moment?" He doesn't hesitate. All the eyes of America watch in anticipation of his saying, "I think it will be when I become President of the greatest country in the world," (or something like that), but he doesn't say that. He says, "I think it was the birth of my twin girls," WOW. He goes on to say that he realized the responsibility and pride that come from having small people looking to him for strength and guidance. He knew those girls for several years to come would depend on him totally for mental, physical, and spiritual support. From that moment on, he would have to be a man of integrity and honor. It made him a better person.

A young Russian girl stands on the floor preparing to defend her honor. Her teammate is leading the floor exercise race to the gold medal. She makes every tumbling pass. She wins the much sought-after gold. The Russian women's gymnastic team took silver in the team gymnastics. In disgust they removed the medals. Silver was not enough for a defining moment. The young Russian girl bows to the crowd in triumph, but no one comes to share her moment. Her coach is working with a male gymnast to prepare for his next event. She walks the aisle looking for someone to share her moment, and finally another Russian girl with poise and style stands to her feet to hug her teammate, to share her victory that had just been taken from her. It is a defining moment.

A young Jewish orphan girl was adopted by her father's nephew. She was raised in Jewish tradition. The king at the time was Ahasuerus. The queen's name was Vashti. Now the king had a big party and got drunk. (I am paraphrasing, of course.) He called for the queen. She refused to go to him. At this time, no one refused

Ordinary Miracles

the king. According to the law, the king took away the crown from Vashti.

This brought about a problem. Who would be queen? All virgins were called to come before the king to find the new queen. The young Jewish orphan girl was very beautiful and very likable. She was taken in by the king's court and adorned for review before the king. All her beauty and charm overwhelmed the king. (What a story, huh? From orphan to queen.) It came to pass (they said that back then) that the king was given the opportunity to see Esther's loyalty.

Someone was going to kill the king, and Mordecai, her adopted father, told her about the plan. She told the king and the coup was demolished. This only heightened the king's affection for his queen. The king appointed a dude named Haman to his court. Haman pushed Ahasuerus into making all bow and worship him (arrogant, huh?).

Mordecai would not worship him because of his Jewish roots. Haman was angered and asked the king to decree that all Jewish people die on a certain day. Mordecai and the Jewish people rent their clothes, fasted, and prayed. Esther caught wind of this because she loved Mordecai and trusted him. She looked for him outside the gate every day. Mordecai had told Esther not to tell the king of her origin. She obeyed her father and did not tell.

Now, doesn't this make for an interesting story? The king has proclaimed innocently to put to death the woman that he loves. Such drama. Queen Esther sends to Mordecai for answers of what to do. Mordecai sends back an answer that horrifies Esther. He tells her to go to the king and have the decree removed. He explains to her that Haman plans to take the throne. This is not a solution to Esther because she cannot go to the king unless he calls for her. She will be killed if she goes to him and he does not raise his gold scepter to hear what she has to say. Esther did not know it, but this was her destiny.

Mordecai knew the words to motivate her to get her blood pumping, to instill the pride that lies deep inside her. He said, "You have been raised to royalty for such a time as this." This is your defining moment. This is the moment you were born for, the time to stand and be a symbol to your people. Esther did go to the king, and the king did raise the golden scepter, and Esther saved her people from destruction.

Jesus in three very distinct words lays out for us His defining moment. He says, "I am come." He did not say, "I have come," or "I will come." He said, "I am come." What does this tell us about him? It tells us that He knew His destiny. He was ready for His defining moment.

None of the athletes that we see at the Olympics stepped up to the vault, or swam, or dove, or ran for the first time. These guys had trained their whole lives for this. They were passionate and relentless about their jobs. They lifted weights, got up at 4 a.m. to go to the pool, sat in solitude studying their form. Their sport had taken their whole lives. They were passionate about what they did. They sacrificed every day to accomplish what would one day be their shining moment.

Jesus lived, lives, and will live for you. You are His defining moment. You are his passion. He spent His whole life to prove that you mean more to Him than the riches of heaven, more to Him than all creation. In those three words, "I am come," He is saying, "I will sacrifice to reclaim the victory. I have come to redeem you. I am willing to burn out my life to save you. This is my defining moment, and I am up for the challenge. I am come." It is not something that Jesus did or will do or can do. IT defines Him. To define means to give meaning to. Jesus defines us. He gives us meaning. I thought He came to save me, but I never realized how deeply passionate He was about it until these three words were absorbed into my thought pattern, "I am come."

Ordinary Miracles

I always wondered how Jesus could stay on that cross through all the torment and pain and not stop it. Now I sorta feel like I have an understanding of that. No athlete stepped up to complete work and stepped away saying this really isn't something I want to do. No, they finished what they started. So did He. With all the pride, joy, and pain he endured what He was born for. He saved you. He took you back. He defined every moment. In the lowliest place, as all of heaven sang the Anthem of Creation. He restored you.

Now you, what is your defining moment? What do you live, breathe, sleep, eat for? What do you wake up wanting to accomplish and go to bed in anticipation of accomplishing? What defines you?

I have news for you. You will have a defining moment. You will step up and decide what your life is for. You can be a symbol to your people. You can change your world. Jesus is all that matters. He has made you and wants you to succeed. He has raised you to royalty for such a time as this. You only have one life. Burn it out with passion for the cause of Christ. You will one day stand in front of your Redeemer and Savior and Father. You will step to the platform as the crown is placed on your head and the Anthem is sung. Tears will stream down your face, and pride will well up in your soul.

You are training now for that moment. The performance has begun. You only have a little while to make a difference, and you don't have to do it alone. Walk in the light. Recognize our kinsmanship — to the Creator. Live life as it was intended. Tony Campolo says, "If there were no heaven or hell, I will still serve Jesus every day because of that love, oh, that love." You are a champion. The last chapter has been written, and you will win because Jesus is come. Because of those three words that ring out for eternity, "I Am Come."

Dorothy A. Day

"I AM WILLING"
Matthew 8:3 Luke 5:13

When I began this incredible journey to find out who Jesus really is, I mean who He said He is, I would never have imagined the three words above, "I Am Willing," to tell me anything about Jesus except that He healed someone. The leper came to Jesus and said, "Lord, if you are willing, you can make me clean." Jesus' response to the man was the focus of this chapter. He looked at the man and said, "I am willing." From this one small phrase came a miracle that changed this man's life forever. What can this phrase do for your life? Let's see.

First of all, let's determine what being willing really is. Webster defines willing as "inclined or favorably disposed in mind: Ready." So, Jesus was saying to this man that He was inclined or ready to make him clean. In other words, it was something He wanted to do. Taking it one step further, Jesus is saying, "I Am ready and inclined to heal your hurts and work miracles in your life. It is part of who I Am."

There is this woman who lives on the streets of Jackson, Mississippi. Her name is Kaye. She has no home except there. You can ask anyone who works downtown about Kaye, and they will know who you are talking about. Most people walk past her in embarrassment, but they all know her. I am ashamed to say that lots of times I don't walk on the same side of the street with Kaye. On those days I am not willing. Some days I am very willing to stop and have breakfast or lunch with Kaye. On those other days I am not willing. Some days I give her money, but sometimes I am not willing.

When I define willing as ready or inclined then I am ashamed that even when I do see Kaye and speak to her, or give her lunch sometimes, I am not really willing. I am doing it out of some obligation or to make myself feel better. Two weeks ago, Kaye was robbed and beaten really badly. She had to be put in the hospital. I have not seen her since. I miss her. I am used to her being there, and she is gone. In the building next to mine they are giving money to Kaye's social worker to help take care of her. Two guys went to see her last week. My mom sent her a drawing pad because Kaye once drew a picture of her that she has proudly framed and hung in our home.

Truth is, if Kaye had been downstairs in her normal place today, I would have been more than willing. I would have been so glad to see her. I would have been inclined or ready. I think today I see Kaye like God sees me and He is Willing. It is not some action that He does. It is an adjective for who He is. He sees me as helpless as I see Kaye, and He hurts when I hurt, just like I hurt for Kaye. All these people who walked past Kaye every day are not rallying around the idea of helping her. She may never know how much these people care for her and even love her. It's probably because we never showed her love. That's what makes Jesus so special. He is always willing.

The second definition for willing in Webster is, "done, borne, or accepted by choice or without reluctance." Matthew and Luke both register this story. Neither of them gives us the impression that Jesus hesitated and thought about it, sighed, and said, "OK." In both accounts Jesus did it without reluctance. He saw the man hurting. He knew He could help. It was His natural response to the situation. It was who He was and is. He is Healer, your Healer and the Lepers' Healer. He is still standing here waiting for you to say, "If you will ... If you will, you can make me clean. If you will, you can make me whole. If you will, you can satisfy my heart." To all of these it is His very nature to say, "I am willing."

I said that being willing was Jesus' natural response to things. I have a friend at work that goes to kidney dialysis every day. With his only having one kidney, the thought of that horrifies me. He is so positive and really a good team player. He name is David. We are broken into smaller teams at work that compete with the other teams. On these smaller teams, we form some very significant relationships. We know about each other's families. We know spouses by name and face from their pictures on the desk. We know each other's likes and dislikes. We eat lunch together almost every day. We could order for the other person. We share the same job frustrations and are growing and developing together.

I am telling you this to tell you that Wayne decided to share his extra kidney with his teammate. Wayne and David are going in for surgery next week. Friday, everyone in our call center that can will be giving blood. I ask Wayne about it. He says, "It's no big deal" which is to say "I am willing, not just going to do it because I get anything back but because it comes natural to me." David and Wayne are brothers who love each other. Other than work they have absolutely nothing in common. Wayne is much older than David. David is African American, and Wayne is Caucasian. I only mention that to say being willing is to eliminate all boundaries and barriers that once existed. Wayne seems to mirror the second definition Webster gives, don't you think?

Webster's third definition of Willing is "of or relating to the will or power of choosing." I know in my own life I can suck it up and do things if I have a choice. Some things I really don't want to do I will do because I have a choice to do it or not. Often, we search for the will of God in our lives. We hear sermons about the perfect will of God. We even pray to find God's will in our lives. I think His will is that we are willing. When we see someone in need, He wants it to be a natural response for us to be willing to help.

When Shawn needs twenty dollars to get his car fixed so he can come to work and I was going to buy a pair of pants with my extra twenty, I think He wants me to be willing. When someone is crying or needing to talk to me and I don't have time, I think He wants me to be willing to take the time. I don't think He wants me to sigh and say "uhhhhhhh, ok." I think willingness should become a part of me because from these three short words Jesus showed that it was part of Himself. Jesus had a choice to skip the cross but His correct response was "Not My will but Yours be done."

It is my prayer that one day I will respond correctly and say, "Not my will, but Yours be done." I think it is possible for us to trade our will for God's, to be so close to Him that His will becomes our first response and not something that we think about. Jesus never questioned God's will for His life because He was close enough to know it. Even when His will differed from His Father's, He still knew His Father's will.

I want to get that close. I want to be willing. What about you?

"I AM ABLE"

I once thought that being willing and being able were synonymous; however, I have realized that you can be willing without being able — and you can be able without being willing. I can't decide which is more important; to be willing or to be able. Lots of times I have been able but not willing; and other times I have been willing but not able. Thankfully, Jesus reminds us in Matthew 8:3 that He is willing. Now, the only other ingredient we need is able.

Well, in Matthew 9:27, Jesus says, "I am able." Wow. What is He really saying? Let's explore further.

I lived in an apartment complex for eight months. During that time, I saw many people come and go. My mom refurbishes furniture as a hobby. She likes old stuff that she can make look new again. Her mom and dad, my grandparents, have a wood-working shop, so she likes to putter around in it. As people come and go, they decide that some of their old stuff has to go, and they chunk it in the dumpster or set it beside the dumpster to be picked up as trash. I have given away a bed to a lady who needed one for her daughter from that pile of rubble. She loved it and was very thankful. She didn't know that it was trash, so consequently she didn't see it as trash. My mom has a chair and end table that she is currently working on.

I told you all of this to say that I recently acquired two beautiful white upholstered chairs that, to me, were a treasure. They were a bit dirty, but they had true potential. I picked up some carpet cleaner and went to work on them. Still a few spots, but I could live with them. I proudly displayed them around my dining room table. Time after time people would say, "Those are beautiful. Where did you get them?" I had to explain that the chairs came from the dumpster to the dining room.

Isn't that a lot like me and you? We spent most of our young lives in the dumpster, cluttering our lives with harmful things and wallowing among the trash. We didn't even know we were getting dirty. It was after we realized that we had made a mess of things that we came to Jesus. He pulled us out of the dumpster and put us in His dining room and began feeding us. I know this because Psalms 23:5 says, "You prepare a table before me in the presence of mine enemies; you anoint my head with oil; my cup runneth over." Isn't that great? He anointed my head with oil much like I did with the chairs. He cleaned me up and set me at His table.

There is more to this story. God doesn't just proudly display us around His table. He continues to perfect us and make us His children. He sends us out to do His good work and bring more children to the table.

We have a small square church. The pews were running east and west. We decided to turn them north and south just for a change of pace. We had a pew sitting behind the pulpit, but when we made the change, we noticed that the church was not completely square. We needed that pew to complete the set-up. That left us without any place for the Pastor and song director to sit. My grandmother asked if anyone had two chairs that matched that did not have arms on them, simply because sometimes visiting pastors may need a little more room than our pastor needs. I stepped forward very proud of my two treasures and said that she could use them. I explained that they had a few spots but were very comfortable. She told me to bring them, and she would look at them and decide what to do. Upon careful examination, she determined that they would work and that she would just cover them, and they would be like new. She said they were perfect for the task.

Now, I don't know about you, but that has very significant meaning for me. From the dumpster to the table — from the table to the pulpit. From junk to God's house. Isn't that just what God has done for me? He has covered me with Jesus' blood and made me like new. He has changed me and made me presentable for the Father. Giving those chairs makes me smile. It is my pleasure.

I am willing, and I am able to do this. Changing me makes God smile. He is willing, and He is able to do this. What an awesome thought. He said it himself. He said He was able. He said He was willing. What an extraordinary combination. Being willing is not enough. Being able is not enough. But being willing and able removes all previous boundaries.

"I AM THERE"

Today is my first day back at work from Thanksgiving Holidays. It has been a wonderful holiday; but, yuck, we are back to our same old routine — kids in school and grown folks at work. Well, we still have a lot to be thankful for. We made it to work today without any incident. We have visited friends and family that we don't see every day. It is really cool that with those people, you can pick back up right where you left off. It's amazing how comfortable that can be. I love work; it's the getting up part that kind of dulls the luster. I also love spending time with you and with my words. You are important to me. Before I finish every chapter, I pray for you, the reader. I pray my unqualified words will find a way to your heart and that Jesus will touch you with them.

Dorothy A. Day

Neatest thing is you don't have to be an author to write. You don't have to have an overwhelming command of the English language or spell correctly or punctuate correctly; you can just be willing, and God will take control. I know this because I am probably the worst speller and not that good with words. God tends to use ordinary people with real weaknesses so He can get through. To me that is astonishing. It overwhelms me. Eli wrote a song, "Unqualified." In the song the chorus says, "I have stolen, cheated. I have lied, I am prideful and unqualified; I am broken when I realize it's God's grace, God's grace that covers me." Wow.

Eli was on the radio this morning talking about that song. He said, "You don't have to be qualified, you just have to be willing. God tends to use the unqualified, but qualifies the called." I will never in my own strength be able to make a complete thought for anyone who reads this, but God can make it make sense to you. Tony Campolo talks about John Wesley when he met Christ for the first time. He wandered into a prayer meeting service. They didn't have a speaker so they read from Luther's Commentary to the Romans. Good reading, huh? John Wesley said, "Never had I felt such fire and joy." Campolo concludes, "God doesn't need eloquence and entertainment." God can use a willing heart. One like yours and mine. Simple unqualified people.

I told you all of this to explain to you what I think Jesus meant when He said, "I am there." Again I think He was sharing with us a part of Himself, part of who He was. "I am there" tells us about the nature and relationship that God affords to us. I am convinced He is there. I realized something this week that I have to share with you. I learned this week that I am angry. It is not something I act out; it is a part of me. It is something I am, a part of me. It is something I need to allow God to remove from my very core. To take upon Himself at the cross and wash it away from me so that it is not my nature but removed. Maybe you can fill in the blank with something you want to have removed from your character. I am

_____. God does have the ability to absorb that into Himself at the cross and remove it from your being.

He can and will, and you know why? Because He is there. I know He is there because He said so. Later we will study, "Lo, I am with you always, even to the end of the age." He is there. He is willing to absorb everything that is dirty and foul about you and me. He is ready to qualify our call and fill us with who He is, removing what destroys us and hinders us from abundant life.

I will call to Him, and He is there. I will ignore Him, and He is there. I will spit in the face of the Creator of the world, and still He is there. Maybe you have never been this rebellious, or maybe you are not yet willing to admit you are; but, regardless, He is there. How do I know? In Matthew 18:20 He tells me so. Now you may say that I am taking these three words out of context and maybe I am.

I know the scripture says, "Where two or three are gathered in my name, I am there in the midst of them." That has so much meaning. I am also convinced that Jesus is there before you even know to call His name. I am convinced that He is there when every baby cries and when every elderly person dies. I am convinced that He sees and knows all heartache and despair and is present through it all. I am certain that He is a gentleman and does not always make His presence known but is only a whisper away. Let me tell you how I know.

I was about 22 years old. I had been to church but was totally unconcerned about God and anything He had for me. I was struggling through life, making it on my own. I hadn't read a Bible verse in years and had no relationship with God. I chose it that way, and I much preferred it that way. I was self-sufficient and thought I was doing a pretty good job.

One day in December about three days after Christmas, I was driving down an icy road trying to get a tire fixed when I swerved to miss another car out of control and spun off a hill into a lake.

The car was filling with water. I had a three-year-old child with me. I looked at her knowing I would never get out of that car but that I had to get her out. She was so little. All of a sudden, I wasn't so big and bad anymore. I couldn't do it all by myself. I screamed, "Oh, God!"

I didn't mean "oh no" or "help." I just wanted to know that God was there. I hadn't spoken to Him in years. I hadn't felt Him anywhere near me. Now, since I am writing this now, you know He heard me. I took a kick at the windshield in my tennis shoes and broke it out. I took my arm and raked the glass and stuck the baby out the hole and said, "Swim." After that for about fifteen minutes I don't remember a thing. The next thing I remember was walking back up a steep hill to a gentleman who carried me back to my closest friend's house to take me to the hospital. Thankfully, the little girl came out with two bruises and a scratch. I on the other hand had lots of time to think about it. My arm was cut. My back had no skin on it and was broken in two places. The bone below my eye was broken, and I would be down for a month. I did not speak to God for a while after that. I didn't even acknowledge that He had saved me. As a matter of fact, I forgot He was there.

Several years passed, and I was going along again on my own. Doing pretty well. I was managing a convenience store making $375.00 a week and proud of it. You couldn't tell me anything. I look back now and believe I was probably terrible to work for. I didn't need anyone's help. I worked about eighty hours a week to make it to the top. I was poised to take over running eight stores. Again, I was driving down the road, this time with a couple hundred dollars going to get change for the store. I was driving a Dodge Colt my grandfather had given me. It was a little car. I say was because you guess right. All of a sudden a tractor cutting grass on the side of the road came right out in front of me. I hit him going about 55 or a few more miles per hour. Again, I remembered my

Ordinary Miracles

Maker. I asked for His help. The accident knocked the breath out of me, and I was gasping for air.

I couldn't breathe. I thought this was it. My life flashed again in front of my face. I got out of the car, holding my chest to check on the tractor driver. I saw him lying on the ground, but he was ok. When I bent over to check on him, blood poured from my face. I realized he was ok, but I was not. The ambulance came and put oxygen on me, and I realized I was not doing well. I called out to God, and He showed up. In the emergency room they let me know that I had a few broken ribs and needed a little surgery on my face and a trip to the dentist to restabilize some teeth but other than that I would be ok.

Now you would think after a couple of major bumps on the head I would have come to my senses, but, no, it just didn't happen.

I finally was very successful in the convenience store business. I purchased one with a few friends of mine. We were really doing well working every day of the week, about 14 hours a day. That can't be good, but, boy, I thought it was. I was on top of the world. I used my settlement from the last accident for the down payment, and away I went. The hours I wasn't working I spent sleeping. I was chasing the almighty dollar with both feet. It was all that mattered. I had all the power and control I needed to do or have whatever I wanted.

That is really not a good idea for someone like me. I am relentless in my pursuits — I just don't quit. I think everyone should work like me, and I don't settle for anything less. All of a sudden, all that changed. I got a phone call telling me Albert Powers was killed. Mr. Powers was a very nice man. My mother was ill with a brain tumor when I was young. She took us to church until she got sick. I was about ten years old. My father did not go with us. Mr. Powers picked me up every Sunday morning after my mother got ill. He ran the church bus route, but he picked me up to help him before he went to get the bus. He made me feel important. I knew he cared about me. His wife and children sorta adopted me into their family through this time period.

Now, probably fifteen or twenty years later he was dead. I couldn't believe it. He was a very young man and, oh, how sad his family would be. I hurt for them. I couldn't stay at the store. I had to leave and go see Debbie. I hadn't left the store in four years during a shift. My grandfather died, and I changed shifts and worked fourteen hours still. I just never left.

This time I had to go. I had to say I was sorry this happened. I had to let them know that I didn't think it was fair. I was so hurt I can't even put it into words. My heart was crushed. I went to the store and bought a ham to hold on to when I walked through the door. I knew it would be terrible. I just had to go even though I really didn't want to. I walked in, and there were hundreds of people there. They were all talking, and I suddenly didn't feel so important or special to him.

I realized he had touched a lot of people just like me. People who couldn't stay away. I saw some people I knew and asked them to tell Debbie how sorry I was that this happened. I asked if she were ok. They assured me she was doing fine. I walked out the door. She came running toward me. She left those hundred people in her house and said the words I will never forget.

She said, "Al would be so glad that you came." She thanked me for coming and said she felt so close to heaven now. She looked at the stars and the birds differently. She was really doing ok. She had a peace that I could not comprehend. It was genuine though. I could tell that. She was not all broken up on the inside either. She was hurting but in a peaceful kind of way. Now I know that she knew God was there. That was part of His nature. She knew He had not left her or forsaken her. She had learned the lesson that two terrible bumps on the head had not been able to teach me.

The next day I took off work again, much to my partners' surprise. They were shocked. Not angry because I worked more

Ordinary Miracles

than anyone else. Not upset because they had to work for me, just in utter shock. I went to the funeral. I was still blown away and was trying to comprehend where Debbie drew her strength. The preacher began the funeral service. The largest Baptist church in Vicksburg, Mississippi, was full and overflowing. The balcony was full, and people were standing in the back. Heathens and Christians alike were lined against the walls, and the preacher spoke.

I hope I never as long as I live forget his words. He was not flashy. He was almost whispering to mask his own tears. He said, "I can just see Al Powers in Heaven today. He is standing with God, and God speaks to him. God says, 'Al, you have two choices today. Choice number one you can go back; next year you can see your daughter get married. The next year you can watch Mike graduate high school. Choice number two. You were a young man when you died. People notice when young men die and maybe one of those people will come to know me and trust me if you just stay here.'" The preacher continued. He said, "Al answered God by saying if someone may come to know you, I will just watch from here." My heart was open to the God that had been there before and who was ever so present then. I accepted Him that day and never looked back at life. My attitude changed, and I found the God of Abraham, Isaac, and Jacob that day. The God of Al Powers and Billy Graham. The God of all who searched for Him and found Him because He had proclaimed in Matthew 18:20, "I am there."

Later that year, my mother died. I loved my mother and yet I was consumed with peace. Again the powers that be allowed me behind the wheel of a vehicle. One month after my mother's death, I was hit head-on by a lady who dropped a cigarette on the floorboard of her car. I again was driving a small vehicle and was terribly wounded. After the car stopped and I knew I couldn't move to get out, I realized the joy of knowing the God I had only hoped would arrive the times before. My Bible had come to rest on my chest after the crash, and a young lady was sitting in the back seat.

I never remember her getting in or out, but she spoke to me and held a rag to my face. She asked if I read my Bible. I said yes and told her if it was time she could read it to me. She smiled and said I would be fine. I felt a warm feeling all around me and I rested in the arms of a God I knew was with me.

I spent several days in intensive care and was lying in a bed two doors down from where my mother had passed away one month earlier. I cannot in earthly terms describe the peace and assurance I had that day. I had found literal rest for my soul. Circumstances were terrible, but God was so there. Since that day, I chose not to sue the lady and lost my portion of the store but gained a brand-new life. Today, life is so much fuller than it was that day. God is so much better than I ever thought He could be. I am never alone, and I know it. I have a new family, new job, new outlook and a very present Savior. I still have my drivers' license, but I bet you wouldn't ride with me, huh?

My little brother Nathan is sixteen, and I asked him to explain the phrase that all teenagers use now. The phrase is simple. It is "I am there." I asked the kids at church if they want to go to the movies and they respond, "I am there." Nathan defined it for me. He said, "It means there is nowhere else I want to be. Nothing in this lifetime could keep me from there."

Isn't that wonderful? Doesn't that sound just like God? When Jesus said, "I am there," He meant that there was nowhere else He would rather be. You had His attention. Nothing could keep him from showing up. It is His desire to be with you. It is the reason He created you and hasn't left you your whole life. It doesn't take a lot of words; He knows your heart. Let go and He will catch you. I am convinced that He doesn't give up on you without a fight. He is there through all the injustices in your life, and His heart is breaking with you.

Did you know that in Jesus you have more power than you can comprehend? Did you know that when you gather in His name

Ordinary Miracles

you invoke power in Him to act? This verse says, "Where two or three are gathered in my name I am there in the midst of them." Remember Shadrack, Meshack, and Abednego? There was a being like the Son of God in the midst of them in the fiery furnace, and they were not harmed.

Power. The day of Pentecost. Power. The Last Supper. Power. Raising Lazarus from the dead. Power. Paul's conversion. Power. Power and love are an unbeatable combination. Jesus tells you He will show up. He promises His presence. He knows how much it will mean to you. You won't ever be left in the street wondering where He is. He is there. Not just in spirit but in the midst. In the middle of things. Working things to the glory of God through you and one unqualified. What a ride!

Now here is the question. Are you there? Is showing up part of who you are? When people are hurt and wounded, are you there? When there is a need, do you show up? Do you bring God's power with you? As a Christian we are called to be Christ-like. That means showing up should be part of who we are. For some people, your showing up could mean the difference in eternity. I am learning this lesson with every punch of the keypad. I am not faithful like God is. I am praying that God will work through me and help me to be faithful to others. Each day is a growing process. As I learn more about God's deity, I am striving to grow to be more like Him. The heart is willing, but the flesh is weak. I love with each "I am."

If you have things in your life that you cannot overcome, go to the one who is willing and able. Travel to the Savior who wants to and can. As I sit and watch the pastor sitting in the chair, I am reminded that all things are possible with God. I am reminded that His love and mercy overcome all previous constraints.

In Matthew 9:27 where the story takes root, we find Jesus and two blind men. The blind men cried out to Jesus. They asked Jesus to have mercy on them. Jesus asked, "Do you believe that I am able to do this?" Simple question, huh? They quickly answered, "Yes,

Lord." Jesus reached out and touched them and said, "According to your faith let it be to you."

Jesus has not changed. He will not change. He can still heal. What if your healing was dependent on your faith? If my emotional and spiritual healing is dependent upon my faith, frankly I am still a little weak. What about you? There were two blind men, blind like we were before we saw Jesus. I trusted Him to heal me, and He did because the scripture tells me Jesus is willing and Jesus is able. I will trust in Him and believe. He will cover me and present me to the Father faultless. He will use me much like that old chair. It is so pretty now. In His eyes I must appear the same way.

What an awesome God.

"WHO DO THEY SAY THAT I AM?"
Matt 16:13-15; Mark 8:27-29; Luke 9:18-20

Who are you? My niece would emphatically stand to her feet and put her two-year-old hands on her hips and reply to this question, "I Tia Hyatt!" Ask people who they are, and they will reply with their names or with none of your business, right?

When I ask the question, I am not looking for such a response. I don't want to know your name or what your nationality is. I want to know about you. Who are you? Really down deep, who are you? What makes you tick? What do you stand for? What do you believe in? What is your purpose for being? Who are you? What do you like and dislike? What controversial subject really gets you rambling? What experiences in your life have made you what you are? Who are you? Who is your family? Where did you come from, and where are you going?

I am interested in knowing the real you!! The part of you that is hidden from any others until you really get to know them and can trust them with that secret part of you. What are your dreams, and how long have you dreamed them? What do you want to do with your life? If today were your last day on earth, how would you spend it? I want to know you. Whose picture is on your nightstand by your bed? What kind of movies do you like to watch? What kind of food do you like to eat? Where do you spend your leisure time? Do you like to sleep late, or get up with the chickens? Do you have a quiet time? Do you like bubble gum? What flavor? Can you run really fast or not at all? Are you emotionally all right? Is there something I can help with? Are your parents still together? Are they still around? Do you get scared sometimes? Are you ticklish? What is your nickname? Are you in love? Where will you spend eternity? Do you know Jesus? Do you like dogs or cats? Is green your favorite color? What kind of car do you drive? What's your favorite worldly possession?

Who are you?

No — down deep, who are you? I really want to know you. I want you to trust me with the real you because we are friends, and I would never hurt you. I want us to be able to finish each other's sentences. I want us to go places and do things because I just already know you like those things. I want to really know who you are. Then and only then can I tell others how truly wonderful you are to me.

Jesus had a friend like that. His name was Peter. How do I know? Three times in the Bible Jesus asked His disciples who the people thought that He was. Their reply was "Some say you are a prophet; some say you are John the Baptist; some say Jeremiah."

Jesus responded with, "But who do you say that I am?" In my mind Jesus was saying that those that did not know Him personally may wonder about Him, but the guys that He ate with, slept with, bathed with, walked with, shared with, mourned with, and taught should know him. They should know that He was for real, that His only agenda was saving them. They should know why He lived and why He was going to die and should know His heart!

He swallowed and asked the question, "Who am I to you?" Peter, knowing His leader and friend, boldly said, "You are the Christ, the Son of the Living God." Imagine how that made Jesus feel? He was so proud of Peter. Peter knew who He was and that He was legitimate. Peter believed in Him. It was that faith and belief that could build a church that the gates of hell could not prevail against. It didn't matter who didn't believe in Him, just that someone did. Doesn't it matter to you that someone believes in you? If your best friend believes in you, if someone who really knows you believes in you, then does it really matter that someone who doesn't know you doesn't? Not as much, huh?

Next Question. Who do you say that Jesus is? You know today, some still say that He is a prophet. Some still say that He was a great teacher of the law. Some say that He was God's Son. Who is He to you? Can you say with Peter that He is your Savior? Can you say that He is your friend? Is He legitimate to you? Do you even know Him well enough to guess who He is? He is standing right there asking you the question. He wants to know you like the first paragraph. He wants to be part of your life. He wants to give you everything your heart desires. If you know Him, you will find that He is your heart's desire. He wants so deeply to enter you because He knows the outside is just a shell of who you are. Inside you are already His child just waiting to reclaim your kinsmanship. All you have to do is reach out to Him, and you will find Him standing before you, saying exactly what He said to Peter.

He said, "Blessed are you, Simon Bar-Jonah, for flesh and blood have not revealed this to you, but my Father who is in Heaven. And I also say to you that you are Peter. And on this rock I will build my church and the gates of Hades shall not prevail against it. And I will give you the keys of the kingdom of heaven and whatever you bind on earth will be bound in heaven, and whatever you loose on earth will be loosed in heaven."

Ordinary Miracles

He is saying to you who know Him now that you are blessed and have all power and authority to build the kingdom of heaven. He has given you everything you need, and the gates of hell cannot stop you!! Wow!! It's worth your time to get to know Him. Know Jesus so well that you are sure of what He would do.

Know who He is. Talk to Him. Share with Him your inner self, and let Him share His with you. It is the ride of a lifetime.

I know who I was without Him, and I know who I am in Him. Believe me, you will like me better now. Jesus is so cool; so available. I see Jesus in my Christian friends.

I guess it all comes down to one thing; Who do you say that He is?

Who is He to you?

"ARE YOU THE ANGEL?"

Josh Dawson

There is a spot in every station that the same people gravitate towards. For me it was a recliner in the center of the room. The recliner, like me, was worse for wear and threadbare. The pleather was worn off most of it. I had been awake for almost 30 hours by now when those all too familiar sounds emanated from my radio. "Medic 1, we need you 10-8 to highway for a single car rollover."

This area was about 25 minutes away which causes a slight panic for my partner and me. This is the middle of the night in one of the most rural areas. There is no help for an hour in any direction, so it's just my exhausted partner and myself. As we make our way down this road made during the Civil War, we are seeing a common sight … nothing. We are traveling at maximum velocity down a two-lane "highway" which was little more than a paved-over stock trail. This was an overshadowed area, but that didn't matter because the clouds covered any illumination that the moon would have given us.

Flashing lights broke through the darkness. Our headlights showed several people waving frantically. This was the scene. This is the place where we were supposed to be.

The roadside has been withered away by time and Mother Nature. She left us with ditches wider than the length of a car and twice as deep. We see the bottom of a car resting at our eye level. It is upside down and pointing towards the ravine which was hungry for its next victim. The car had been stopped by a narrow precipice from flying through the air towards certain death for everyone involved.

As the reality of the scene struck my partner and me, our fatigue faded quickly. My mind went into "rescue mode." This was a common event I have become used to. The floodgates of adrenaline begin to open which cause all the senses to magnify to an almost supernatural level. I was suddenly aware of the crispness in the air. Normally it would be welcome but for someone losing blood, cold can be a death sentence.

I turn to my partner. He's an old hand in prehospital medicine and a veteran of two wars. I turn to him and ask for him to get us "help." As he is working the radio and phone determined to get the resources we need, I scale these sheer walls. Normally a person whose body looks like a science experiment in poor eating habits would never be able to move down one side without the aid of gravity, much less up the other side. Adrenaline has now become my closest ally.

As I rise to where the car is, I discover that the car is resting on the knife's edge of this precipice. The top is only around 3-4 inches wide. It's not even wide enough for me to stand, but somehow it was enough to stop two tons of steel and glass. There are two voices emanating from the compartment that was once a cabin. The first person, with wide eyes, asked, "Are you the angel?" I disregarded this question. I had more pressing issues to remedy right now.

I am now into the second stage of my scene size up. The first occurred when we arrived at the chaos. The second is now focused on how many people were victimized and how to get them away from the danger. The first patient was relatively close by. That look of terror was one that I was quite familiar with, seeing it countless times before. *Ok*, I say to myself, *time to be a duck on the water.*

I have to display a calm and peaceful face while my thoughts are paddling like a duck on a pond. I took the patient's hand and gave it a steady but strong tug. It was just enough strength to take her from this death trap to the safety of solid ground without causing more injury.

As the first patient exits the car, the car rocks. This is the worst thing that can happen right now. This metal demon now has shown that it's willing to dive headlong into the gully I just crossed or the infinite darkness of a 100-foot fall in the other direction. The danger has now leveled up. I hear the desperate notes of a thin voice inside the car, but I also hear the roar of a new noise. There is a fire truck screeching to a halt behind my ambulance. I hear a shout from the operator: "Medic, what do you need?"

"Everything" would be the best response, but this situation needed more specifics.

"Grab your attic ladder and make me a bridge." My partner, who was still on the road, scrambled to dislodge the longest ladder stocked on the fire truck.

The technique is simple. You extend a ladder where both ends are around a foot longer than the edge and then secure it with whatever you have. This ladder was not quite enough to do that. I hear voices from the valley that were causing so much havoc. There were bystanders and police officers.

"Where did they come from?" I asked myself.

"I don't care" was my answer. I looked at the other half of my team, my partner, and said sternly, "Make it work."

As I'm redirecting my attention to the car, there is another shake. I instinctively throw my leg through the open window to hold the car in place. This would be about as successful as a tick stopping a river, but I had to do something. The rescued patient is holding my shoulder to steady herself and asks again, "Are you the angel?" I didn't answer but now am evaluating her mental state.

Is she having hallucinations? Is this a head injury or shock that's causing this question?

I don't have the time right now to check either of these. I have to focus on the task at hand which is to get these two people away from the danger.

There is a tap on my foot. A police officer and a willing bystander have climbed the valley and secured our makeshift bridge. I look at my free patient and give them instructions on how to get her out of this place and to safety. The two men are helping direct her, and my partner awaits. She's across, now time to get the other one.

Unknown at the time, this was going to be even more difficult. This person is truly trapped. The bones of the leg have been wrapped around the steering wheel and she is not within arm's reach. I make the choice to crawl to her through the mangled steel and broken glass. As I'm moving into the car, I start telling everyone that the most important task right now is to stabilize the car.

As I crawl to the face of terror, I hear movement and clunking. Ok, let's get an IV in this arm. I still don't know what arm I was working with, but the IV was in and flowing. Pain management was next on the list. Pain can cause plenty of secondary issues, and for this situation we don't need any more. I give just enough to keep the patient conscious for what comes next, the unwrapping of the leg. Screams pierced my ear, and my soul became bruised because I knew she was screaming from what I had to do. The leg was free! The next obstacle was in sight.

We had to get this person out of there. Unlike the first one, this one couldn't help. As I mustered up all the strength I had then, my shoulder was tapped. One of the police officers had joined me on the peak. Now we are a team on this mountaintop. I had a small sigh of relief. I scramble to the edge of the peak leading me under the car. The car had been secured with every type of contraption that could have been mustered. Redneck engineering at its finest.

The officer was halfway into the car when I arrived at the other side. Together we lifted with the coordination of an ice-skating team. The patient protested in screams, but the task was done. We moved her to the bridge and then the roadside. Safety was achieved, and the immediate threat was neutralized.

On the ride to the hospital my first patient asked again, "Are you the angel?" She was completely coherent and physically fine. I now take the opportunity to ask why she was asking me. She looked at me with a fearful expression. She said, "I heard the crash and felt the car begin to careen from the road. I saw a man standing under the car holding it against the hill. He smiled and then was gone."

In the aftermath my partner and I returned to the scene. The car was still in place, and the tow truck driver was devising a way to bring it back to the road. He asked what had happened and we gave him a brief synopsis. He said, "What did y'all hook up to the bumper?"

I told him that I didn't know because I was focused on other things. When we were able to examine this thing that used to be a car, we saw marks to the front. There were two bends in the straightest part of the car. The bends were shoulder width apart and the size of hands.

I wasn't the angel the young person saw. What she saw was a real angel, who by the grace of God, stopped this tragedy from becoming fatal.

WHAT'S IN YOUR HAND?
Dot Day

Are you a worker of ordinary miracles?

Are you ever asked, "How can I help you?" Or told, "Let me know if I can do anything for you."

I become a deer surrounded by headlights as I search for an answer to these sincere requests.

How do you ask for anything without thinking how much greater the burden placed on others?

But, if we all consider what's in our hands, many can share in easing the burdens.

Carl is such a one. An almost octogenarian, she cleans the house of her daughter-in-law, an invalid, each Thursday. Time together — priceless. The ministry, a chore, is often painful for her arthritis. Did she have time to add anything else? She lives in an older Victorian-era home perfect for entertaining. Recently she invited those in attendance at church to join her for her New Year's Day meal.

She and her friend Dot, a true octogenarian, take meals from church fellowships to a shut-in. The two of them put up my Christmas tree and decorated inside the house for Christmas. Both have brought us so much more as they visit, often with food in their hands.

What's in your hand? What do you have to give?

Becky knows of an invalid who likes lemon candy. She stops by to visit bearing candy. She regularly takes another woman to two of her three weekly dialysis appointments with no recompense.

Some of you find yourself with scissors in your hand, snipping off stray pieces of hair. Dot is one who shows up with basin, pedicure equipment, and scissors. When an invalid needs toe nails tended or hair shortened, she has made herself available.

After a disaster, children still need toys and a sense of others' love and compassion. Lynn leads in an effort to supply such a token. Ashley and Sandra have willing hearts and hands to be personal shoppers for those who cannot shop. Paula collects items of practical use: toiletries for those whose homes were destroyed by a recent tornado and food for a food pantry.

What's in your hand?

Food? So many meals from friends. My husband does not find cooking, baking, planning meals, or learning to do these things on his bucket list. However, circumstances have reached the point that these are now his responsibilities. Betty comes with chicken and dumplings; Charlotte's offerings vary and are frequent; Dena makes the best marinara sauce; Becky or Jeri come with "crack chicken."

Tammy and Reggie supply eggs; Elizabeth shares a Saturday morning feast with homemade fried pies; Carl's corn bread or any salad garners our attention readily. Sonny and Cece's pepper sauce provide the perfect taste in vegetables.

Today we have a power outage. Although we use a generator, we don't use the .220 current that powers the stove. It would deplete the gasoline. Barbara and Bruce have a Generac that runs on butane. She called, saying, "I'll be over in fifteen minutes with your lunch — I made poppy seed chicken and butterbeans." Yes, this is the same Barbara that now does most of my typing and lots of other things.

When Charles, my cook, my caregiver, my husband, was ill, we were in dire straits. He helped me transfer from my motorized wheelchair to the commode. His strength did not last for the return trip back into the chair; he and I both fell. After the fall he was able to get himself up. We called on neighbors to assist. Over a two-day period, Cody, Roy, Cecil, Kathy, and the 911 ambulance crew helped lift — him, twice and me, twice. Once prior, Charles and our neighbor Wesley performed the lifting miracle.

I outed these helpers on Facebook, an easy answer to thank-you notes. Alumni from Copiah Academy came bearing frozen casseroles, delectable soups, only requesting I let them know when we needed help. Other friends sent money for our daughter Sharon to buy whatever we might need. She and Stephanie, also our daughter, spent the rest of the week filling in as caregivers and allowing their father to rest.

Again, what's in your hand?

Our small church is made up of a mixture of ages, but an abundance of those who are older than 65. I am being kind with those words. It is a 75-year-old who sets up the banquet tables and plans the food and the decor. Jeri also lent us the use of her freezer.

The sanctuary altar table frequently has new bouquets of flowers provided by Lucille, another octogenarian. For a church workday she made five dozen biscuits, and then she was the one outside trimming the hedges on a very cold day.

Jim is another nearing 80. Despite his working a 40-hour week, he is faithful to attend all church services; Saturdays he is actively and intentionally sharing the plan of salvation to others in the parking lot of a local store.

For several months, Eddie ministered to those in prison. He and Phyllis provide a home for a young adult with nowhere else to live. My friend Tammy pens community and church updates for the local newspaper.

When our church wanted a youth minister, the now-retired pastor Dave gave part of his salary. His wife, Trish, our pianist, gave up all of hers.

Only our daughters and Wendy have been daring enough to drive our kneeling mini-van with all the attachments to keep my chair and me legally in place as we travel. With her many abilities and her servant's heart, it's not a surprise that Wendy's son is a missionary in India!

Again, what's in your hand?

One of my sisters, Lurlene, worked her way from two strokes to picking up her crochet hook — baby blankets, caps for cancer patients, afghans. The other sister Maxine stays ready to purchase anything she thinks I might like or need. They and Co-Lin (community college) girls regularly pray for us.

Numbering from twelve to thirty, depending on the size and need of the church, a group of us would descend on a church to share current testimonies of what God was doing in our lives. These lay renewals, led and organized by Sid and Mary Lou, were gifts to the host churches. The farthest distance for Charles and me was Harrisburg, Pennsylvania.

I taught English for 25-plus years; I know how to construct and de-construct a sentence, even an essay. I have been learning how to write, however, through a critique group of writers: Gerald, Hazel, Janet, Lottie, Patricia, Reni, Reva, and Terry have shared their writing and their wisdom.

So many writers and AUTHORS have trusted me to use some of their stories in this book or in *Battles: Glimpses of Truth*.

Again, what's in your hand? What do you have to share?

I have been so blessed to teach and to learn from my students and my clients. Susan is one who has faced several illnesses (She has had breast cancer, spot on lung, spot on pancreas; after the major surgery on the pancreas, she fell and broke her hip.) and shares a strong faith (Next Breath, Heaven!). She has told Charles to let her know if there is anything I want to eat; she can cook it. She regularly supplies us through her family restaurant.

Sweet Barbara Roper sent a lovely bouquet for my birthday. The Soul Sisters, particularly around the Queens' Cove area of Bolton, have sent me bottles for a bottle tree (greatly desired and furnished a couple of years ago by Sharon), zinnias, pecans, casseroles, pecan pies, and included me on some of their fun trips.

Sisters Marcia and Melody came bringing a fabric tote made by Melody filled with all kinds of goodies.

Jeri helped clean out and organize my writing area after Charles had put together a desk in the back bedroom/now office.

I requested some of my friends to let me know of anyone willing to come to our home to type for me. Barbara G. responded, "Will I do?" Considering she had taught business classes, I hastily agreed!

One of my college roommates has been known to use Facebook to spread the word, "The Back Porch will be closed Sunday." My imagination lets me think of a group from church or her neighborhood pooling Sunday lunch. Charles will not eat in restaurants on Sundays because he knows doing so will mean workers will not have the opportunity to attend worship services.

So many organizations are dependent on volunteers. The churches and communities would be vastly different without those willing to serve.

I hear regularly from my daughters. Sharon, my college roommate Rachel, and I post our *Wordle* results daily. Sharon is busy, but I know she's okay when I hear the early morning notification. Stephanie and I have an extended talk usually on Friday but always at some point during the weekend. Do you have a phone?

Mr. Rogers reminded us of the importance of helpers. Can we lighten the load for someone else? Cut a neighbor's grass? Baby-sit?

What could you do if you were willing to be an ordinary miracle worker?

> Think of the needs around you.
> What's in your hand?

CONTRIBUTORS OF
ORDINARY MIRACLES
Writers of Stories, Tellers of Tales, and Poets

Dot Barker: "Heather's Miracle" "Lula's Memories of Childhood"

Lottie Brent Boggan: "The Christmas Gift," "Tippy Toe Dreams"
Lottie Brent Boggan has a knack for finding humor in the worst of circumstances. She's been a long-time contributor to the Northside Sun, a weekly newspaper in Jackson, Mississippi. Lottie has had numerous accolades, winning The Eudora Welty novel competition, placing at the Faulkner Wisdom Competition, and receiving newspaper column awards. In addition to her novels, she has also compiled multiple anthologies of short stories and served as editor to several critically acclaimed authors besides herself. She was a founder of The Red Dog Writers and is a member of Middle Mississippi Chapter of the Mississippi Writers Guild, The Jackson Chapter of the Mississippi Writers Guild, and Mississippi Gulf Coast Writers Association.

Lottie's family is somewhat of an icon in Mississippi, with her father having started Brent's Drugs, which was featured in the movie, "The Help." Her late husband was a founder of River Oaks Hospital, now Merit.

Dorothy A. Day

Heather Bouchillon: "Heather's Miracle"

Gwen Shows Bouldin: "Hard Candy Christmas," "Grandma's Quilts," "Grandpa and Trixie," "Patterns."

Ashley Chisolm: "End of August"
Ashley Chisholm was born in Greenville, Mississippi, and reared in Gallman. As a Social Work graduate from Belhaven University, she worked several years in West Jackson as a community outreach and children's development director. She now owns an Etsy shop that helps kidney failure patients find donors and co-owns a digital media production company, alongside her husband, where they primarily produce documentaries and commercials. She currently lives in Crystal Springs with her husband R.D. and three dogs.

Bill Clark: "Merry Christmas, James — Wherever You Are," "Addendum, Big Heart."
Bill Clark: Entertainer-Pianist-Crooner-MirthMaker-Impresario-Consultant-Facilitator
Since high school days in the Free State of Jones, Bill Clark has spent much of his extracurricular life creating music, smiles & laughter. Along the way he has worked in television, radio, print, political consulting, sales and marketing, and plain 'ol hoss trading; his mother's maiden name having been Hoss.
From his years in television, he is best remembered as the spokesperson for Brandon Furniture — a furniture store which operated (if you will) in an abandoned hospital in Brandon, Mississippi. He created a pseudo-personality which he named Dr. Brandonne' Furnechur — an imaginary character who was his alter ego and co-spokesperson.
In his younger days his high school and college group, The Cee Jay's, won sweepstakes at the MidSouth Fair Youth Talent Contest in Memphis and appeared on the Ted Mack Original Amateur

Hour in New York. Bill has entertained at innumerable banquets, luncheons, pageants, and other events. He has also been active in Baptist circles in music and otherwise.

In 2011, Bill began a semi-annual musical variety show The Musical Extravaganza. The show features top-notch Mississippi talent and draws attendees from all over the state and region. In the ten years since the show started well over 12,000 people have attended.

He is an Alumnus of The University of Belhaven where he was active in student life and served as president of the Student Government. In his retirement years you will often find him on the 88's at a luncheon, dinner party, or venues as diverse as The Governor's Mansion, an airport hangar, or the popular restaurants Table 100 or Char.

Bill and his wife, Jean, live in the Flowood/Brandon area and have three daughters; Christi, Kim, and Julie, who (thankfully) live in the metro area with their families.

His mantra is — Stay in the Game!

Contact Info:
601-750-2364
billclarklive@live.com
www.billclarklive.com

Jasmin "Jas" Clark: "Congratulations, You Won! Prize Patrol" "Wait a Little Longer" "What's your Favorite Cup of Tea?"
Jas Clark was born and reared on a country farm in Simpson County, Mississippi. She had her best loved ones teaching her about the Lord and trying to keep her off a colorful path. She lost each of them — her daddy, her mama, and especially her sweet granny. She retired from teaching school and then taught kindergarten. This got her ready for her next journey, taking care of her mother. After spending 10 years taking care of her mother with

Alzheimer's, the Lord started giving her memories every morning from her loved ones in heaven. She states, "I feel life does not build by only positivity but also through the hardships. I guess folks call hardships negativity. Hardships teach you to appreciate the beautiful moments of your life and see how much the Lord blesses us. The Lord gave me a quote, 'I'm a sinner trying to do better.'"

Madalyn Clark: "Motivational Analysis: Dorothy Day"
Madalyn Clark received her Bachelor of Science degree in psychology from Mississippi State University in 2020. In fall 2023 she will be a graduate assistant at the University of Southern Mississippi as she works toward her degree in marriage and family therapy.

James Davis: "An Act of Selfless Love"
James Davis has retired from an employment standpoint, but he has not retired from life. He maintains his home, yard, vehicles, and a booth in a consignment shop and still finds time to post daily a devotion on Facebook and an online newspaper, The Magee News. He is active socially and busy with church and family events. James was from Waynesboro, Mississippi, but moved to Magee and graduated from Magee High School. He received both bachelor's and master's degrees from the University of Southern Mississippi. His teaching career involved stints as senior English teacher at Harrison Central High School and Mendenhall High School, and he was adjunct English professor at Copiah-Lincoln Community College. He had a second career in federal service, serving as a Congressional aide to U.S. Senator Thad Cochran. He has one son, Jamie, and two grandchildren, London and Landry, recent high school graduates.

Josh Dawson: "Dispatch, Medic One! We Need You, 10-8" "Are You the Angel?"
Josh Dawson worked as a paramedic in Mississippi for seventeen years before moving on in June 2023 to become the manager for the Mississippi Department of Health's EMS Department. He certified for both neonatal resuscitation-NRP-and the critical care transport service — CCEMTP. He and his wife Jessica live in central Mississippi.

Dot Ainsworth Day: "I Remember" "Singing of Self" "Spring Nonsense" "Big Heart" "Big Heart, Too" "The Dress" "Fall #47" Love of the Game" "Sleep, Blessed Sleep" "I Choose Us" "The Tin Whistle" "Playing Church" "Dear Courtney" "A Dog Moves In" "How my Dog Saved my Sanity" "Therapy Lady" "Tele-Phony" Next Breath, Heaven" "What's in Your Hand?"
Dot is a retired (because of late-onset muscular dystrophy) teacher and family therapist. Follow her at mississippiwriterspathways. com
http://authorcentral.amazon.com/gp/profile
dotday@bellsouth.net

Janet W. Ferguson: "Hagar"
Janet W. Ferguson is a Christy Award finalist, Maggie Award Winner, and the FHL Readers' Choice Award winning author of realistic inspirational fiction. An avid reader, she loved books so much she found a job as a librarian so she could be around them all day. Then she turned that love of story into writing faith-filled novels with characters who feel like best friends. You'll laugh and cry as the quirky heroes and heroines chase their happily ever after.

Janet and her husband live in Mississippi where they say y'all a lot, and she forces him to visit the beach as often as possible. They have two grown children, one really smart dog, and a cat that allows them to share the space.

Dorothy A. Day

> FHL Readers' Choice Award Winner
> Christy Award Finalist
> Maggie Award Winner
> Selah Award Finalist
> Bestselling Inspirational Author

John M. Floyd: "Della's Cellar"
John M. Floyd is the author of more than a thousand short stories in publications like Alfred Hitchcock's Mystery Magazine, Ellery Queen's Mystery Magazine, The Saturday Evening Post, Best American Mystery Stories, and Best Mystery Stories of the Year. A former Air Force captain and IBM systems engineer, John is an Edgar Award finalist, a Shamus Award winner, a five-time Derringer Award winner, and the author of nine books. He is also the 2018 recipient of the Short Mystery Fiction Society's lifetime achievement award.

Barbara Grillot Gaddy is a retired educator and communications manager. She earned her Master of Education degree with certifications in Business and Computer Education from Mississippi College in Clinton, Mississippi, and taught at high school and community college levels. Barbara was recruited by Ingalls Shipbuilding in Pascagoula, Mississippi, to develop their Computer Education Program, instructing employees in software applications, networking administration, and mainframe data transfer. Her subsequent positions at Northrop Grumman/Ingalls Shipbuilding included Information Technology Program Manager for various Ingalls functional business organizations as well as Manager of Information Technology Communications. She is married to Bruce Gaddy and has three grown children.

Courtney Harris: "Live Sent"
Courtney Harris is a 2021 graduate of the University of Alabama, earning a Bachelor of Science in psychology with a minor in personal wealth management. She lives and works in Tuscaloosa. She is a customer service associate with the wealth advocacy department of a credit union.

Lauren Harris: "Power to Choose" "Narrative"
Lauren Harris is an Interdisciplinary Studies major at the University of Southern Mississippi. She plans to use her degree to teach performing arts and mathematics.

Caryl Hackler: "My Grandmother's Love"

Carl Heard: "Beyond Belief"

Averyell A. Kessler: "Silver Dollar Day," "Fear Not," "Behind the Garage" "Deep Roots," "Ezekiel Saw the Wheel"
Averyell Kessler is a native of Jackson, Mississippi, who lives in an aging house surrounded by the requisite white picket fence. She welcomes homeless dogs, wandering cats, and even a family of hoot owls living in the magnolia tree in her front yard. After retiring from the peace and quiet of a lengthy legal practice, she's taken up writing in hopes of finding additional peace and quiet. A dedicated bibliophile, she welcomes books as carefully chosen kin and takes pleasure from the soft scratch of turning pages, the slight aroma of paper and ink. She is wife, mother, grandmother, and now writer.

Education: Louisiana State University, BA in English: Mississippi College School of Law, Juris Doctorate, Cum Laude. Publication: Mississippi Magazine; The Ponder Journal Literary Magazine, Mississippi University for Women; Columnist, The Northside Sun, Jackson Mississippi, Our South Magazine; Epis-

Dorothy A. Day

copal Café e-magazine; On-line blog with over 3,000 readers Employment: Associate, Perry, Morrison and Smith, Attorneys at Law; Associate, Low and Furby, Attorneys at Law; Marketing and Publicity, W. Kessler Ltd.

Hazel R. James Lonie "~~Cinquain~~: Sensory Poems"
Hazel R. James Lonie — "Writing is one of my favorite hobbies. My writing started about two years after my mother's death. This therapy allowed me to verbalize emotions I couldn't talk about and hide within my writing. I have been able to exact the gravity of situations and realize the humanness in others and myself. Retiring from Jackson Public Schools with twenty-eight years of service, I taught art and tutored math and reading. There are times when I miss the hustle and bustle of teaching. Then I come to my senses and realize I'm not able to meet the demands of a full-time job."

Larry McAlpin: "Mission Accepted"

Carl Merchant: "Spiritual Heart Condition"

Cindy Mount: "Love"
Cindy Mount, a lover of God, wife, mother of two, and Nana of seven grandchildren was born in Beaumont, Texas, but reared a Louisiana girl, a Southerner for sure. Cindy has been married for 42 years, works part-time, and shares her love for God wherever He opens those opportunities. Her spiritual roots started sparsely but through years of experiencing life's ups and down, her roots have grown deeply into the spiritual soil of Scripture and a relationship with God. She has been an avid journaler for over 30 years.

Janet Taylor-Perry: "Seven Years Out" "Illusion! Epiphany Proclamation!" "Layers of a Painted Life" "Stomach Staples and a Cyclone"
Janet Taylor-Perry: Like many of her characters, Janet is a history buff and loves anything of historical significance from old cars to old cemeteries. Get to know Janet:

http://www.janettaylorperry.com/
http://janettaylor-perry.blogspot.com/
https://authorcentral.amazon.com/gp/profile
https://www.facebook.com/
Author-Janet-Taylor-Perry-299698950061301/
janettaylorperry@gmail.com

and you'll see why she's been critically acclaimed at the Faulkner Wisdom Competition and why her writing continues to receive 4- and 5-star reviews — It could be that readers see so much of her in her characters: mother, educator, author, editor, and a person who has overcome great obstacles and still holds on to her faith.

Rita Floyd Purser: "You Can't Make It on Your Own"
Rita F. Purser and her husband Eugene live in Star, Mississippi. They have two children and three grandchildren. They are active in church activities. A graduate of Magee High School and Copiah-Lincoln Junior College, Rita also has a Bachelor of Arts degree in Business Administration from Belhaven College, Jackson, Mississippi. Before serving as secretary to the President of Wesley College, she accumulated 32+ years' experience in the legal field, including experience as a legal secretary, office administrator, and paralegal.

Dr. Bob Rich: "A Different Christmas Tale" "Paddy's Story"

Dr. Bob Rich, Ph.D. earned his doctorate in psychology in 1972. He worked as an academic researcher and applied scientist until retiring the first time at 36 years of age. Later, he returned to psychology and qualified as a Counseling Psychologist, running a private practice for over 20 years. During this time, he was on the national executive committee of the College of Counselling Psychologists of the Australian Psychological Society (APS), then spent three years as a Director of the APS. He was the therapist referrers sent their most difficult cases to. Bob retired in 2013, but still does pro bono counseling over the internet. This has given him hundreds of children and grandchildren he has never met, because many of these people stay in touch for years. His major joy in life is to be of benefit to others, which is why he wrote a book that's in effect a course of therapy. He has been an environmental activist since 1972, because he had young children and wanted a good future for them. Now, he has grandchildren and great-grandchildren and works for at least some chance of survival for them. He has authored 19 books. You can get to know him well at his blog, Bobbing Around, https: //bobrich18.wordpress.com

Pauline Rule: "The Musings of Pauline" — "I Am Come," "I Am Willing," "I Am Able," "I Am There," "Who Do They Say that I Am?"

Pauline Rule is the Chief of Staff, Compliance and Integrity Operations at AT&T Integrity Operations in Jackson, Mississippi. Her past roads led her from acquisitions agent, 1st level call center manager, performance development coach, area manager to her current position. She notes two pieces of memorable advice: "Never forget what it was like to take your first call" and "Be yourself — you are good enough." She uses her position to influence others to own the mission of living the company's four culture pillars. She works toward creating leaders. She earned a Master's degree from Clairmont Lincoln University. Within the past year she lost eighty pounds by riding a bike!

Gail Harvey-Walker: "Have You Ever"

Gail Harvey-Walker: "I am a native of Copiah County, Mississippi, born in 1966 at Hardy Wilson Memorial Hospital in Hazlehurst, Mississippi. My particular disorder is Arthrogryposis which causes bones to be fused at the joints. Any joint can be affected, but in my case, it is my knees. I also had a club foot, drooping eyelid, hip dysplasia and a mild case of scoliosis. I spent the first few months of my life in a body cast, crying from daylight to dark.

Fortunately, I was born into a family that loves me unconditionally. I was also blessed with a huge independent streak and a (mostly) happy disposition. I'm not going to lie and pretend my life has always been perfect, because I have had many days when I've wondered why I am here. However, over the years I've come to accept and love myself, and now I try to share some of my knowledge about life and love with others.

I'm grateful and thankful for the love and support my family has given me throughout my life. My son Jacob Walker is the greatest gift ever. He has stood by me through the darkest of times.

Printed in the USA
CPSIA information can be obtained
at www.ICGtesting.com
JSHW010744020923
47462JS00003B/6